The Ghost of Meter

The Ghost of Meter

Culture and Prosody in
American Free Verse

Annie Finch

Ann Arbor

THE UNIVERSITY OF MICHIGAN PRESS

In memory of my great-great-aunt
Annie Hughan
And my great-grandmother
Annie Ridley Crane Finch

First paperback edition 2000
Copyright © by the University of Michigan 1993
All rights reserved
Published in the United States of America by
The University of Michigan Press
Manufactured in the United States of America
♾ Printed on acid-free paper

2003   2002   2001   2000   4   3   2

A CIP catalog record for this book is available from the British Library.

Library of Congress Cataloging-in-Publication Data

Finch, Annie, 1956–
     The ghost of meter : culture and prosody in American free verse /
Annie Finch.
          p.   cm.
     Includes bibliographical references.
     ISBN 0-472-10405-5 (cloth : alk. paper)
     1. American poetry—History and criticism. 2. Free verse—History
and criticism.   3. English language—Versification.   I. Title.
PS309.F7F56   1993
811.009—dc20   93-22341
                                                                      CIP
ISBN 0-472-08709-6 (pbk. : alk. paper)

Preface to the Paperback Edition

Since the initial publication in 1993 of *The Ghost of Meter,* the controversial idea of the metrical code has not fitted easily into existing critical approaches. My argument occupies an unusual position within contemporary schools of thought regarding poetics, prosody, literary history, and literary theory. The occasion of the publication of the paperback edition of my book inspires me to attempt to clarify the extent and scope of my original argument, alerting readers to what they may and may not expect from this method of interpreting poems.

The metrical code is a way of interpreting the metrical lines in free-verse poems. It provides a new way of approaching poetic history and influence within those free-verse poems that engage with meter. The intriguing question of how consciously or unconsciously poets made the metrical choices discussed here, while well worth exploration, remains outside the scope of this book. For the record, my working hypothesis has been that metrical choices in free verse arise from the intuitions of the poet's rhythmic unconscious in interaction with the collective poetic unconscious preserved by literary history. Whether or not my hypothesis is true, the level of consciousness of metrical choices should have no significant effect on metrical-code readings.

Because of the metrical code's self-reflexivity, we can infer the attitudes that certain poets or groups of poets held toward specific meters. By extension, we can then speculate on larger poetic movements and how they developed. For example, metrical code readings in this book suggest that not only dissatisfaction with the iambic pentameter but also attraction toward triple rhythms set the stage for the twentieth-century free-verse movement (see pp. 64–66). Alienated, perhaps, by the nonrepresentational nature of meter, some recent critics have feared that the metrical code reduces or essentializes poems to metrical features. To the contrary, metrical-code readings do not replace, but complement, the meanings we already discover in poetry through structuralist, deconstructive, historical, and other approaches.

The metrical code is best understood as a literary-historical rather than a prosodic argument. Much contemporary free verse, including the majority of texts that now fall under the general rubric "Language poetry," is free of even brief passages in meter (and, increasingly, even of lineation itself), so the notion of a metrical code applies only to a small segment of free verse. It works in tandem with prosodic approaches to scanning free verse: systems that involve line breaks, rhythmic phrasing, syntactical units, or other features that characterize free verse generally. However, some critics have faulted it either for failing to provide a complete free-verse prosody or, in the words of Marjorie Perloff, for treating [all] "contemporary free verse as essentially a fruitful quarrel with meter" (87). By definition, the metrical code cannot apply to all free verse or propose a new prosody for free verse. It employs traditional scansion in order to pick up traditionally metrical lines—and hence the cultural associations those lines, *by virtue* of being in traditional meters, bring to the poems that contain them.

The study of prosody is at best a contentious field, and even straight-forward metrical poems may be open to multiple scansions. When the poem in question is in free verse and there is no metrical context as a guide, scansion becomes yet more subjective. Skilled readers will be aware of alternate scansions for some of the passages discussed here. The idea of the metrical code rests less on agreement about the scansion of individual instances as on the overall recurrence of metrical patterns that carry related connotations.

The metrical code differs from other aesthetics-based approaches in that it is fundamentally descriptive, not evaluative. Its aim, like that of historical-based criticism, is to understand the poem in a wider context of social and literary forces. Critics sympathetic to formalism have understood this book to argue that "the best free verse necessarily emerges from an engagement with metrical tradition" (Walzer 29), but I do not intend the metrical-code readings in the book to provide a standard for judging the quality or accomplishments either of individual free-verse poems or of the free-verse movement generally.

The Ghost of Meter is a poet's attempt to explain how and why certain meters feel the way they do to poets themselves. Because of the wordlessly self-aware nature of metrical-code readings, the metrical code provides a rare tool for apprehending that aspect of poetic meter that may be hardest to put into words: the relation between word and rhythm, form and content, metaphor and metonymy. To illuminate the small subtleties and vast complexities intersecting in a passage of metered language is a clearly circumscribed task, but one with implications well worth exploring.

Annie Finch
Cincinnati, Ohio
February, 2000

Selected Bibliography

Adams, Stephen J. "Review of *The Ghost of Meter.*" *Canadian Review of American Studies* 25, no. 2 (1995): 142–45.

Dolin, Sharon. "Arguing Poetry: How Contemporary Poets Write About Poetry." *AWP Chronicle* (Dec. 1996): 9–13.

Gwynn, R. S. "Proseurs." *The Sewanee Review* (Winter 1996): 142–49.

Holder, Alan. *Rethinking Meter.* Bucknell University Press, 1995. 116–19.

Maio, Samuel. "A Meter-Making Argument." *Sparrow* 61 (Fall 1994): 52–56.

Marsh, Alec. "Review of *The Ghost of Meter.*" *Boston Book Review* (August 1995): 1–3.

Meier, Franz. "Review of *The Ghost of Meter.*" *Anglia: Zeitschrift fur Englische Philologie,* 1996. 292–96.

Morris, Timothy. "Review of *The Ghost of Meter.*" *Style* (Spring 1994): 125–27.

Perloff, Marjorie. "After Free Verse: The New Nonlinear Poetics." *Close Listening: Poetry and the Performed Word.* Ed. Charles Bernstein. New York: Oxford University Press, 1998. 86–110.

Ponick, Frances. "Review of *The Ghost of Meter.*" *Edge City Review* (January 1995): 42–45.

Walzer, Kevin. *The Ghost of Tradition.* Brownsville, Ore.: Story Line Press, 1998. 25–26, 29–33.

Walzer, Kevin. "The Ghost of Tradition: A Review of *The Ghost of Meter* and *A Formal Feeling Comes* by Annie Finch." *Eclectic Literary Forum* (December 1994): 59–60.

Acknowledgments

I would like to thank the Stanford Humanities Center and the Mabelle McLeod Lewis Memorial Fund for support of this project. I would also like to acknowledge *PMLA,* where the second chapter first appeared in slightly different form.

Thanks are due to the many people who helped me develop my ideas for this book, in particular Penelope Laurans and John Hollander at Yale, and Diane Middlebrook, Paul Kiparsky, and Kristin Hanson at Stanford. My warmest gratitude goes to each of them; for Diane Middlebrook's unswerving and imaginative support I am especially indebted. For ideas or encouragement at various times during the writing process, I would also like to acknowledge my appreciation to Marjorie Perloff, David Halliburton, Jay Fliegelman, Albert Gelpi, Kenneth Fields, Bill McPheron, Marie Borroff, Timothy Steele, and Dana Gioia.

I am grateful to LeAnn Fields of the University of Michigan Press. Finally, I want to thank all the people who loved and inspired me personally during the writing of this book. There are too many to name, but I will mention my parents, Roy Finch and Margaret Finch, and my son Julian, born with the first draft. The most thanks of all are for my husband, Glen Brand, for his continual support and loving help with every stage of the writing of this book.

Excerpts from *The Complete Poems of Emily Dickinson* edited by Thomas H. Johnson. Copyright 1929 by Martha Dickinson Bianchi; Copyright © renewed 1957 by Mary L. Hampson. By permission of Little, Brown and Company.

Excerpts from "The Love Song of J. Alfred Prufrock" and "The Waste Land" in *Collected Poems 1909–1962* by T. S. Eliot, copyright 1936 by Harcourt, Brace, Jovanovich, Inc., copyright © 1964, 1963 by T. S. Eliot, reprinted by permission of the publisher.

Excerpts from "East Coker," "The Dry Salvages," "Little Gidding," and "Burnt Norton" in *Four Quartets,* copyright 1943 by T. S. Eliot and renewed 1971 by Esme Valerie Eliot, reprinted by permission of Harcourt, Brace, Jovanovich, Inc.

Selections from *The Black Unicorn,* Poems by Audre Lorde, are reprinted by permission of W. W. Norton & Company, Inc. Copyright © 1978 by Audre Lorde.

Excerpts from *The World of the Ten Thousand Things* by Charles Wright. Copyright © 1990 by Charles Wright. Reprinted by permission of Farrar, Straus & Giroux, Inc.

Contents

I caught the sudden look of some dead master
Whom I had known, forgotten, half recalled
    Both one and many; in the brown baked features
    The eyes of a familiar compound ghost
Both intimate and unidentifiable.
—T. S. Eliot, "Little Gidding"

Introduction

This book explains and illustrates a new idea about the relation between meter and meaning in poetry, the metrical code. It proposes that meter can constitute a crucial aspect of the meaning of poems written during times of metrical crisis—periods of deep change in the prosodic foundations of poetry. The words in such poems comment, on one level, on their own meter, just as meter enriches the meaning of the words. Metered lines of metrically variable verse can reveal the poet's attitudes toward the meter's cultural and literary connotations.

The metrical code also offers a new way to analyze a writer's relation to literary history and to understand the development of free verse and thus modern and contemporary poetry. Following a central thread in the development of free verse, I explore the role of traditional meters in the metrically variable verse of Dickinson, the free verse of Whitman, Stephen Crane, Eliot, and the contemporary poets Audre Lorde and Charles Wright. Because meters gain meaning from literary, prosodic, and sociohistorical contexts, relevant background in these areas accompanies the discussion of each poet.

Chapter 1 traces the genealogy of the metrical code. It is the most thorough history of ideas to date about the meanings of meter in the English-language poetic tradition. Chapter 2 explains the metrical code in detail and justifies it theoretically, using Dickinson's poems as a text. Feminist theory offers a useful starting point for conceptualizing Dickinson's attitude to the canonical meter, iambic pentameter. Dickinson's iambic pentameters appear in basically metrical poems, rather than in free verse, unlike those of the other poets discussed in this study. As a result, the interplay between iambic pentameter and its prosodic context is especially clear in her work.

Chapter 3 discusses the poetry of Whitman, extending the analysis of iambic pentameter associations and introducing another metrical mode that is significant throughout the rest of this study: the basically triple rhythm that I call, for convenience, *dactylic* (a discussion of this terminology appears on pages 39–40). Whitman developed connotations for the dactylic rhythm that persist throughout the rest of the nineteenth and into the twentieth centuries. His poems also occasion the introduction of two additional general concepts: the *embedded pentameter* and the *metapentameter*.

Chapter 4, an analysis of the poetry of Stephen Crane, opens with a discussion of the importance of triple rhythms in English and American poetry of the late nineteenth century and the ambivalence toward triple feet in criticism of the same period. Readings of Crane's extremely arhythmic poems extend metrical-code analysis to the level of the foot rather than that of the line. This chapter also introduces a subplot of the study, the development of free verse. It treats the possibility that the tension between iambic and dactylic rhythms in the late nineteenth century was a major factor in the emergence of free verse.

Chapter 5 traces the rise and fall of the first widespread wave of free verse in the early twentieth century, illustrating the extent of uneasiness with free verse by the time Eliot published his major works. This history offers one explanation for the success of Eliot's prosody, and serves as background for the analysis of his poetry. Eliot's use of iambic pentameter and dactylic rhythms evolves dramatically in his major poems, from an initial ambivalence toward both meters and the literary influences they represent, including that of Whitman, to simultaneous reconciliation with both meters in his last major poem, *Four Quartets*. Chapter 6 traces some recent prosodic developments in free verse, focusing on the work of Audre Lorde and Charles Wright, and suggests how the metrical code relates to contemporary poetics.

Chapter 1

Meter, Meaning, and the Metrical Code

While the metrical code combines elements from two earlier theories about meter and meaning, it differs from them in its emphasis on the expressive significance of traditional meter within individual lines of poems.[1] Previous critical thought about the relationship between meter and literary meaning may be categorized into three general theories:[2] the theory of propriety, the idea that certain meters inherently suit certain poetic themes or genres; the iconic theory, the idea that meter can reinforce a poem's meaning at particular points by adding expressive sound effects or by emphasizing particular words; and the frame theory, the idea that a meter constitutes a meaningful "contract" with the reader by evoking prior poems in the same meter.

The most ancient idea about meter and meaning in the Western tradition is the propriety theory. It holds that certain meters have inherent meaningful qualities suitable, or unsuitable, to particular kinds of thematic material. A historical overview of this idea can begin with Plato. Socrates, drawing an analogy between music and meter in the *Republic,* asks Adimantus to tell him which poetic rhythms suit a noble life: "what those rhythms would be, it is for you to tell us as you did the musical modes." When Adimantus is unable to say, Socrates continues, "We will take counsel with Damon, too, as to which are the feet appropriate to illiberality, and insolence or madness or other evils," and which for the opposite states of mind (645b–c).

Aristotle's implicit explanation, in the *Poetics,* of why certain meters are appropriate to certain literary situations explains little: the phenomenon is a result of "nature." Aristotle notes that, as soon as speaking parts were introduced in tragedy, the meter changed from trochaic to iambic as "nature herself found the appropriate metre" (1449a). Discussing narrative poetry, he claims that "nature herself . . . teaches us to select the meter appropriate" to epic (1460a). In another passage he suggests, through the phrase "assigned it from experience," that metrical roles developed through cultural practice over time, but even here the appropriateness of the meter is fundamentally self-evident: "As for [the meter of epic], the heroic has been assigned it from experience; were anyone to attempt a narrative poem in some one, or in several, of the other metres, the incongruity of the thing would be apparent" (1459b). Such metrical meaning appears implicitly to combine precedent [frame theory] with rhetorical effectiveness [iconic theory], although the writers who developed the propriety theory do not explain why or how meters derive their essences.[3]

Later classical writers continued to discuss which meters were appropriate for certain genres and rhetorical purposes. Arthur Glowka's essay "The Function of Meter According to Ancient and Medieval Theory," which offers a rare history of the development of ideas about meter and meaning, notes that Longinus contrasts the dactyl, which he considers fit for noble subjects, with other metrical feet such as pyrrhics and trochees (101). Quintilian "recommends the avoidance of trochees in argument, which give speed at the loss of force, but the use of dactyls and paeans for lofty passages and iambs for violence" (102). These writers emphasize rhetorical effectiveness more explicitly than do Plato and Aristotle, but they still assume, in Glowka's words, a self-evident "generic propriety" (102).[4]

The association of certain meters with certain modes persisted throughout the medieval period, as Glowka observes, but with a new emphasis on moral significance:

The emotional power granted to rhythm by the ancients gains moral importance for medieval theorists when they see the capability of meter or rhythm to affect the motions of the soul, the center of sensation and cognition. A good rhythm can turn a soul to God; a bad one can send it to Satan . . . theories of *mimesis* (imitation) and decorum required styles of language to suit both the moral and social aspects of subject, scene, and character. (100)

Such attention to metrical decorum led to insights anticipating the later development of the iconic theory of meter. The sixth-century grammarian Priscian, for instance, argues that the metrical substitutions in Terence's plays are admirable because they match meter to character. Terence's naive or confused characters are likely to speak "in confused rhythms" (Glowka 104). In Priscian's observation, the propriety theory of meter begins to shade into the iconic theory. There is a thin line between the idea that a confused rhythm is morally suitable for a confused speaker and the idea that such a rhythm effectively expresses the speaker's character.

Prosodists of the English Renaissance continued to understand particular poetic devices as appropriate vehicles for certain moods or themes. Gascoigne's "Certayne Notes of Instruction" (1575) concludes with an exhaustive list of prosodic/thematic correspondences.

> As this riding rhyme serueth most aptly to wryte a merie tale, so Rhythme royall is fittest for a graue discourse. Ballades are beste in matters of loue, and rondlettes moste apt for the beating or handlyng of an adage or common prouerbe: Dizaynes and Sixaines for short Fantazies: Verlayes for an effectual proposition, although by the name you might otherwise judge of Verlayes; and the long verse of twelue and fouretene sillables, although it be now adayes vsed in all Theames, yet in my iudgement it would serue vest for Psalmes and Himpnes. (56–57)

Like the ancient writers, Gascoigne does not offer much explanation for his associations. He gives his own judgment as support for the last statement, but otherwise assumes that all these correspondences are obvious. Similarly, Sidney, comparing quantitative and accentual-syllabic prosody in "The Defence of Poesie," assumes that metrical difference entails some self-evident difference in appropriate content. The quantitative meter is "more fit lively to express diverse passions, by the low or lofty sound of the well-weighed syllable" (207).

Eighteenth-century prosodists considered meter to have deep moral implications. Regular meter possessed the power to control the mind and regulate the passions. As it had in the Middle Ages, meter's moral appropriateness verged on iconic meaning. Paul Fussell notes that meter at this period was thought to constitute "a revelation of [the poet's] ethical and religious state" (*Theory of Prosody* 44). Poets of the period also explored the iconic effects of meter for purely artistic reasons, as in the famous passage from "An Essay on Criticism" where Pope simultaneously discusses and embodies iconic metrical devices:

> The *Sound* must seem an *Eccho* to the *Sense*.
> *Soft* is the Strain when *Zephyr* gently blows,
> And the *smooth* Stream in *smoother Numbers* flows;
> But when loud Surges lash the sounding Shore,
> The *hoarse, rough Verse* shou'd like the *Torrent* roar.
> When *Ajax* strives, some Rocks' vast Weight to throw,
> The line too *labours,* and the Words move *slow;*
> Not so, when swift *Camilla* scours the Plain,
> Flies o'er the unbending Corn, and skims along the Main.
>
>   (155)

Samuel Johnson was critical of Pope's tour de force, noting that in the lines about Ajax "there is no particular heaviness, obstruction, or delay," and that "why the verse should be lengthened to express speed [in the last line], will not be easily discovered." He used this passage to exemplify his skepticism about iconic metrical variation, since Pope's effort embodied "what can be expected from the most diligent endeavors after this imagery of sound" (*Rambler* 92, 129). But Johnson also recognized the possibility that iconic meter could add a level of artistic value to poetry in addition to its moral function. He considers Virgil not "less happy in this than in the other graces of versification" (*Rambler* 92, 125), praises the use of "representative versification" in a line by Cowley ("Life of Cowley" 62), and lists several examples of iconic variation from Milton that he considers effective (*Rambler* 94, 140–41). In the section on "Prosody" in his *Dictionary,* however, Johnson makes no mention of the semantic potential of variations from the metrical norm and writes only of "the variations necessary to pleasure" (qtd. in Paul Fussell, "Note" 433).

The pleasure principle, or the aesthetic dimension of metrical variation as opposed to the iconic dimension, remained dominant in prosodic theory throughout the nineteenth and early twentieth centuries. George Saintsbury, the most influential writer on prosody of the late nineteenth and early twentieth centuries, is known for his pioneering tolerance and admiration of numerous kinds of metrical variation and substitution. Saintsbury's praise of skillful metrical variation, however, rests on aesthetic grounds—the ability of metrical changes to alleviate monotony, to "swell and raise [the] rhythm" (*Historical Manual* 110). René Wellek places this attitude in the context of Saintsbury's more general separation of form and content:

> [Saintsbury] resolutely divorces form from content, manner from matter, and often roundly condemns the subject matter while praising the form. . . . He proposes a strange mental experiment: "It must be a singularly feeble intellect and taste that cannot perform an easy dichotomy of metre and meaning. . . . You pour the poison or the ditchwater out; you keep and marvel at, the golden cup." (418)

Early twentieth-century writers on versification continue Saintsbury's focus on the aesthetic function of metrical variation, although they sometimes recognize the possibility of iconic meter. W. Winslow Hall's 1911 *English Poesy*, for instance, treats the subject of metrical irregularities in a chapter entitled "Poesial Variation: The Charm of Ordered Lawlessness." Hall praises various foot substitutions in Shakespeare with terms like "delightful," "a refreshing change," and "a relief from the tameness of invariable decasyllabics" (37).[5] Twenty years later, R. F. Brewer's *The Art of Versification* treats the entire subject of "Imitative Harmony" in a short final chapter, just before the bibliography. This chapter discusses a few instances of iconic metrical variation among the treatments of alliteration, assonance, and consonance. Only one or two statements can be construed as metrical analysis (e.g., Tennyson pictures "the sense of chill cheerlessness by . . . harsh rhythm" [277]). Clement Wood's 1940 *Poets' Handbook* values metrical variation because it gives a sense of "natural conversational rhythm" (159), and advises aspiring poets to "vary constantly from the goose-step of the pattern scansion. Scan your own verses, and make sure that this variance is usual in them" (161). Like Saintsbury's aesthetically appealing rhythm, this varied conversational rhythm is an end in itself, with no iconic function in specific lines.

The theory of iconic metrical variation gained prominence with the development of the New Criticism in the United States in the thirties and forties. The new analytical literary theory, with its focus on the autonomous literary text, entailed more scrutiny of metrical variation. Some New Critics explicitly analyzed the iconic effects of specific metrical variations at length, and the iconic theory of metrical meaning was central to the theory of the interdependence of form and content in poetry. Brooks and Warren's influential textbook *Understanding Poetry* (1938), "one of the chief means of introducing literature students to the close reading techniques and formalistic values of New Criticism" (Shucard, Moramarco, and Sullivan 224), treats metrical iconicity as a basic poetic device. In exercises at the ends of chapters, students are asked to apply the iconic theory to poems: "Scan lines 42–52 of 'Lucy Gray.' Is the metrical pattern in these lines used effectively to support the rhetorical pattern?" (134). "Scan lines 39–42 of 'Preludes.' How does the metrical effect support the meaning here?" (138). Brooks and Warren's readings of poems abound with such observations as "the heavy pause after *silence* gives the effect of the speaker's meditating a moment" and "this heavy emphasis on *long* fortifies the meaning of the word" (118–19). Having gone full circle from Saintsbury, they chastise severely a poem in which "the metrical pattern is emphasized, apparently, as an end in itself" (115).

By midcentury, the iconic theory was so established that Northrop Frye notes, in *Anatomy of Criticism,* that "most of [the imitative devices] in English are too familiar to need recapitulation here: beheaded lines increase speed, trochaic rhythms suggest falling movement, and so on" (98). Paul Fussell's popular *Poetic Meter and Poetic Form* (1965) lists as givens three basic "principles of expression through metrical variation": spondees "can reinforce effects of slowness, weight, or difficulty," pyrrhics contribute to effects of "rapidity, lightness, or ease," and "an unanticipated reversal in the rhythm . . . implies a sudden movement . . . or a new direction of thought, a new tone of voice, or a change or intensification of poetic address" (42).

One distinctive modification of the iconic theory appears in Antony Easthope's 1983 study, *Poetry as Discourse.* Easthope discusses meter's implications from a political and social perspective and treats the iambic pentameter tradition as a whole, not just the meter of individual poems or kinds of poems. Easthope's linking the physical nature of iambic pentameter to cultural meaning carries the iconic theory to its ultimate conclusion, analyzing the metrical pattern itself rather than variations from it. According to Easthope, iambic pentameter evens out intonation along the length of the line, forces slow, formal, controlled pronunciation, and encourages "syntagmatic" thinking because it allows syntax to cross line breaks. All of this contributes, in his view, to the formation and maintenance of the bourgeois personality and aids in political repression. Easthope, whose theory remarkably resembles Samuel Johnson's idea that meter regulates the passions, emphasizes the importance of meter's iconic function in forming no less than in expressing the self.

The iconic theory is open to criticism on the same grounds as other kinds of formalism. The analysis of metrical iconicity can seem subjective or even arbitrary, since metrical effects may derive their meaning from the reader's knowledge of the words of the poem. On the other hand, if meter is thought to have meaning completely apart from the words, iconic readings run the risk of naive, mystical essentialism. As evidence for the latter point, I. A. Richards in *Practical Criticism* presents a metrically accurate imitation of Milton's "On the Morning of Christ's Nativity" in nonsense words beginning "J. Drootan-Sussting Benn . . ." On the evidence of this poetic "double or dummy," Richards points out that accepting the collaboration between meter and meaning is more reasonable than trying to ignore it:

> Such arguments . . . do not tend to diminish the power of the sound (the inherent rhythm) *when it works in conjunction with sense and feeling* . . . so much mystery and obscurity has already been raised around this relation by talk about the *identity* of Form and Content, or about the extirpation of the Matter in the Form, that we are in danger of forgetting how natural and inevitable their cooperation must be. (220–22)

D. I. Sims makes the same point when he observes that to consider rhythms as having meaning separately from the rest of the meaning of the poem "is the way to unhappy frenzy" (352). Reuven Tsur, recognizing that iconic meter may become a self-fulfilling prophecy—"the same meter may interact in different poems with different elements . . . but it will always 'admirably' suit the quality of which it is a perceptual condition"—develops a more sophisticated model of the relation between rhythm and meaning; he discusses the "combinational potentials" of metrical, syntactical, and thematical elements in poems (416). John Crowe Ransom, notorious for his skepticism about the iconic theory, claims that belief in the iconic function of "the phonetic effect in a poem . . . is almost completely fallacious" ("Wanted: An Ontological Critic" 38).[6]

In spite of its problems, the iconic theory continues to influence poetics, and research in poetics, more than any other idea about metrical meaning. Marina Tarlinskaja's statistical analysis of "rhythmical deviations" shows that certain semantic categories occur at a definitely higher frequency in conjunction with metrical variations (27). She suggests a significant alteration in traditional iconic theory, postulating that metrical variations have become associated with their particular meanings through literary convention and are not inherently expressive (30–31). Mark Jacob leaves open the question of whether meter "can be called, in any meaningful sense, semantic" (92). Nonetheless he remarks, for instance, of a line in Pushkin: "it can hardly be an accident that the line which describes the coach's accident occurs . . . at the moment of a breakdown in a fundamental law of rhythmic structure" (89). F. K. Diering claims that "once a basic meter has been established, any deviation from it may become rhetorically significant" (39); in D. H. Lawrence's "Piano," for example, "the rhythmic effect is closely allied to the meaning and supports it" (37).

The most significant contemporary theory about the relation between meter and meaning, the frame theory, was developed most fully in two essays by John Hollander, "The Metrical Emblem" (1959)—since expanded and retitled "The Metrical Frame"—and "Romantic Verse Form and the Metrical Contract" (1965).[7] The frame theory arose at the time in literary criticism when rhetorical considerations about the interaction between writer and reader began to supersede formalism. It emphasizes the importance of the knowledge and previous associations a reader brings to the meter of a poem. "To analyze the meter of a poem," according to Hollander,

> is not so much to scan it as to show with what other poems its less significant (linguistically speaking) formal elements associate it; to chart out its mode; to trace its family tree by appeal to those resemblances which connect it, in some ways with one, in some ways with another kind of poem that may, historically, precede or follow it. (*Vision and Resonance* 162)

The "metrical contract" between poet and reader is based on such family resemblances.

Hollander refers to the romantic period as a "metrical crisis," a period when "it appears that the contract of meter has been broken." Not surprisingly, he develops the frame theory most fully in relation to romantic verse form (202–3). In fact, the frame theory's first foreshadowings occurred at the beginning of the romantic period, a time of wide metrical experimentation and distance from established metrical traditions. These factors may have led to greater awareness of the historical and cultural aspects of meter among the Romantics themselves. In the "Preface" to *Lyrical Ballads,* Wordsworth notes the historical implications of meter. One aspect of metrical effect is "the blind association of pleasure which has been previously received from works of rhyme or meter of the same or similar construction" (150).

When Hollander refers to metrical conventions as a poem's "less significant (linguistically speaking) formal elements," he refers to a distinctive characteristic of the frame theory, its focus on consistent poetic elements whose significance has rarely been acknowledged. Hollander points out that metrical conventions tend to be "ignored or treated at best as an unexamined *donnée,* a given condition," since "within the framework of information theory, it is certainly true that the more surprising event is the more significant one." In the analysis of poems, however, the opposite is often true, and "conventional events are of major importance" (*Vision* 139). The frame theory's focus on meter's conventionality leads to analysis of poems on the basis of initial metrical choices. Hollander's discussion of Blake, for instance, centers on the literary implications of Blake's use of the alexandrine as a metrical frame.

With the recent interest in cultural criticism, Hollander's idea of the metrical frame has grown in influence. Two doctoral dissertations of the 1980s make use of the idea for widely differing purposes. James Shapiro's prosodic analysis of Marlowe's metrical style includes a discussion of the ways in which Marlowe's extension of the range of dramatic blank verse established "a new metrical contract for blank verse" (64). In a more extended treatment of the theoretical implications of particular choices of verse forms, Kevin Lewis examines Blake's fourteener and Auden's tetrameter couplet in view of the historical associations of those meters.

The metrical code is intimately related to the frame theory, since it concentrates on meter as a cultural artifact that evokes previous literary associations and relates a poem to a poetic lineage. Like the iconic theory, however, the metrical-code theory interprets special cases rather than conventions, analyzing the interaction between meter and meaning line by line or even foot by foot within a poem. Within the long and growing tradition of free verse, traditional metrical patterns are no longer conventional events; they are rare and surprising, and have significance "within the framework of information theory."

As distinct from the metrical frame, the metrical-code theory concentrates on the information value of specific occurrences of metrical patterns within a poem. The word *code* implies that meter in a metrically organic poem can function like a language, carrying different information at different points within a poem. Since semantic content interacts differently with meter from line to line or passage to passage of the same work, metrical associations create their own layer of literary meaning as they develop throughout a poem. Like other aspects of poetic meaning, a metrical-code pattern is relevant in at least three contexts: it can add to the meaning of a particular poem, add to the understanding of the development of one poet's work, and illuminate the relation between one poet and another.

Perhaps most importantly, the metrical code also sheds light on what is to me the essence and raison d'etre of poetry: the mysterious connections between speech patterns, the body's memory of rhythm, and the individual and cultural unconscious. In his study of metrical development during the Renaissance, John Thompson proposes that, from the very beginning, to write effectively in accentual-syllabic meter involved an awareness of the gap between language and meter (152). The metrical code depends on the manipulation of meaning, in one apparently self-referential line of poetry, across this subtle gap.

While it is possible that simultaneous echoes of other meters may evoke metrical-code associations in metrically regular poems, this study concentrates only on free verse and metrically variable poems—the two kinds of poems in which meters are available for expressive as opposed to strictly conventional purposes. Theoretically, the metrical code can apply to the work of metrically flexible poets in any tradition, but the strength and continuity of free verse in the United States over the past hundred and fifty years make American poetry a particularly appropriate subject for metrical-code readings.

Chapter 2

Dickinson and Patriarchal Meter: A Theory of the Metrical Code

Emily Dickinson's metrics are an area of remarkable tension. Methodologically as well as chronologically, her work offers an especially good starting point for a study of the metrical code in American poetry. Iambic pentameter is apparent in few of Dickinson's poems, but it structures the metrical identity of those poems and adds its singular force to some of her best-known works. Because of her unusual historical position and passionate, involved poetic struggle, Dickinson is an ideal subject for the study of how meter encodes information about a poem's relation to contemporaneous influences, traditions, and societal attitudes and to the poetic past and its supporting social structures.

Dickinson's poetry offers an appropriate text within which to examine iambic pentameter as a meaningful code because she chose this highly connotative meter only occasionally and unpredictably. Critics have often noted and discussed Dickinson's use of the ballad or hymn stanza, but they have paid little attention to her use of iambic pentameter, due to an inadequate understanding of the cultural and historical resonances of this meter.[1] Critics such as Sandra Gilbert and Susan Gubar who have studied the relation of female writers to a male tradition have laid the groundwork for a useful hermeneutical approach to what iambic pentameter may "mean" in Dickinson's poems. Iambic pentameter codifies the force exerted on Dickinson's poetry by patriarchal poetic tradition (she associates the meter with the power of religion and public opinion, with formality, and with stasis), and her handling of it demonstrates her attitudes toward that

tradition (she resists the meter, approaches it with tentative ambiva-
lence, and sometimes gains power from it).

It is generally accepted that the choice of a particular meter con-
stitutes a relation with tradition, which can carry different implica-
tions in different poems, and that the abstract models of metrical lines
can be more or less altered in arguably "expressive" ways within
poems. But the possibility that a meter like iambic pentameter in
itself functions as an expressive force within poems has not yet been
seriously considered, for two reasons: the relative dearth of metrically
varied texts before this century and an inability to gain enough dis-
tance from the accepted standard to view that meter as one of many
systems. Russian formalist criticism, the work of Roland Barthes,
and contemporary feminist criticism have all contributed in turn to
overcoming the latter obstacle.

The concept of meter as crucial, not incidental, to a metrical
utterance obviously underlies the metrical code. The Russian for-
malists' understanding of poetic form, summarized by Boris Eichen-
baum in "The Theory of the 'Formal Method,'" is that it is "not
contrasted with anything outside itself—with a 'content' which has
been laboriously set inside this 'form'—but, understood as the genu-
ine content of poetic speech" (127). This perception is fundamental
to my study. In fact, since meter is a factor in all poems (even, one
can argue, in those where it seems absent), while subject matter, or
"content," changes frequently, there may be more logic in the pro-
posal that content can shed light on what a particular meter means to
a poet than in the standard notion that meter illuminates content. For
example, Auden ends his famous free-verse poem about the apparent
inconsequentiality of great events, "Musée des Beaux Arts," with
these lines:

> and the expensive delicate ship that must have seen
> Something amazing, a boy falling out of the sky,
> Had somewhere to get to and sailed calmly on.
>
> (237)

In this poem, the ship that sails on in the final line can be read as
a metaphor for the dactyls that tell about it and for what they stand
for. The dactyls connote the classical epics and oracles, composed in
dactylic hexameter, and suggest a framework that might once have

existed for writing about the miraculous subject of the poem—the fall of Icarus—in an appropriately heroic manner. But to Auden's modernist and socialist viewpoint the dactyls, like the heroic sensibility of the poems associated with them, are "expensive" because they depend on a political and economic framework incompatible with ideals of social justice. Auden also finds them "expensive" because of the poetic energy that would be required to find and believe in a heroic ideal in 1938 and "delicate" just because the existence of an epic sensibility is contingent on historical circumstance. The ship, the meter, and the attitude of the first great poems of our culture sail calmly out of Auden's poem, despite the image of the boy who has fallen by flying too near to the sun. The whole poem's comment on art acquires a new pathos when read in the light of this aspect of its final line, the most regular dactylic line in the poem.

It is important to maintain the distinction between this type of reading, which does indeed reveal possibilities in a poem's "content," and the more familiar iconic or stylistic method. A reading process that interprets metrical strategies as significant in their own right helps us to understand the poem as part of an intertextual field and to appreciate its qualities differently from the way we would, for instance, if we read the evocative dactyls as contributing directly to the expression of the ship's departing nobility. The latter reading confines the "meaning" of the dactyls to a particular image, while the former justifies a reading of the whole poem in relation to this meter.

As Juri Lotman remarked about the metrical line, scansion "not only . . . permit[s] us to feel that there *might be* a stress at this point [the point where the metrical pattern has led us to expect it] but brings out the fact that it *is not there*" (46). If the different structural levels of the poetic text are "in a state of contrastive comparison [and] form a structural paradigm both on the supraphrasal and supra-lineal levels" (Lotman 155), then the same principle should apply to a poem as a whole: one metrical line can inform a whole free-verse poem with its absence, as in the Auden poem. The rest of the "Musée des Beaux Arts," it can be argued, demonstrates dactylic absence when read in conjunction with the last line in the same way (though inversely) that the spondees in Lear's "Howl, howl, howl, howl! O, you are men of stones," in conjunction with the meter that dominates the play, show iambic absence. While in Auden the distinctive line affects all the rest and in Shakespeare the regular iambic pattern affects the two feet that are different, the most highly connotative meter in both works, present when it is absent, affects the parts of the poem that lack it. Instead of reading meter as yet one more expressive tool used by the poet to refer to an extrapoetic reality, the metrical-code theory sees meter as part of the reality to which some poets, consciously or unconsciously, refer.

An account of Barthes's idea of codes in *S/Z* demonstrates their appropriateness as a framework for describing the meanings of meter:

> each code is one of the forces that can take over the text (of which the text is the network), one of the voices out of which the text is woven. Alongside each utterance, one might say that off-stage voices can be heard: they are the codes: in their interweaving these voices (whose origin is "lost" in the vast perspective of the *already-written*) de-originate the utterance. (21)

The metrical code may function in poetry, and possibly in prose, as essentially as do the hermeneutic, semic, symbolic, proairetic, and cultural codes developed by Barthes in *S/Z*. The metrical code would function in some situations like the proairetic code, adding a narrative tension, though below the surface, to lyric utterances; sometimes like the cultural code, by evoking the authority of metrical tradition; and even like the symbolic code in poems where meter, instead of serving as a tool, actually "effects the structuration of the text" (Barthes, *Grain* 76). While any of these functions can predominate in a poem, meter gains its initial significance through cultural connotations. Meter can be "used" in the same way that artifacts and actions of all kinds are constantly appropriated and turned into mere signs of themselves within new sign systems, a process Barthes describes in *Mythologies*. Iambic pentameter, dactylic hexameter, or any other standard meter served to tell past readers that certain pieces of writing were poems, a codification John Hollander terms "the metrical contract" (*Vision* 195). Such meters have accumulated meanings that poets can exploit as a semiological code. Combined with a mythological (to Barthes, bourgeois) consciousness, lines in these meters do not communicate only their apparent meaning as they did when they were full "signs" (both signifiers and signifieds); insofar as they are metrical each serves instead as signifier of a signified concept like "epic sensibility," "traditional poetry," or "patriarchal poetry." The tension between the meter as mythic signifier and the line's words, which do function as a complete sign, makes the two meanings comment on each other as they do in "Musée des Beaux Arts" and many other free-verse poems.

Hollander has noted that William Blake accompanied his rebellion against the restraints of his culture with unrhymed seven-foot lines ("fourteeners") in an "attempt to create an anti-meter, as opposed to the norm of blank verse" (*Vision* 206). Other poets, from the romantic period on, have equated metrical freedom with freedom of content and associated formal meter with artificial, anachronistic, or backward-looking restrictiveness. In general these poets have either loosely employed a regular metrical line, as Hollander notes of Blake, or completely abandoned rhymed accentual-syllabic verse in favor of a freer metric based on speech cadence, syntax, new units of rhythm, or the logical, imagistic, or emotional "content" of poems. Emily Dickinson, in her resistance to the authority of a standard meter, used strategies that differ both from those of the revolutionary male English-language poets Blake, Smart, Hopkins, and Whitman and from those of twentieth-century free-verse poets. The idea of a metrical code illuminates some of the historical pressures on her work and clarifies some of her resultant poetic tactics.

By Dickinson's time, iambic pentameter had been in standard and nearly uninterrupted use for five hundred years. Milton's blank verse in *Paradise Lost* had given iambic pentameter an even heavier weight of authority than it had carried after Chaucer, Spenser, and Shakespeare. According to Harold Bloom, Milton, "the great Inhibitor, the Sphinx who strangles even strong imaginations in their cradles" (*Anxiety of Influence* 32), has impeded all but a few exceptionally strong subsequent poets from asserting themselves, and those poets have achieved their identities only by struggling with their precursors in an oedipal father-son confrontation.

In *The Madwoman in the Attic,* Sandra Gilbert and Susan Gubar discuss the ways in which Bloom's model clarifies the difficulties female poets experience:[2]

> For Western literary history *is* overwhelmingly male—or, more accurately, patriarchal.... On the one hand ... the woman writer's male precursors symbolize authority; on the other hand, despite their authority, they fail to define the ways in which she experiences her own identity as a writer. (47–48)

Gilbert and Gubar posit that female poets have experienced not the "anxiety of influence," which a strong poet such as Keats could convert into a profitable oedipal "misreading" of Milton (in Bloom's terminology), but the "anxiety of authorship," because of fears that "authority" of any kind is by definition inappropriate to women (51). The problem for poets is exacerbated by Milton's misogynistic cosmos, in which,

> as a male poet justifying the ways of a male deity to male readers he rigorously excludes all females from the heaven of his poem except insofar as he can beget new ideas upon their chaotic fecundity. (211)

According to Gilbert and Gubar's model, women writers have traditionally struggled out from the double bind of the "anxiety of authorship" by disguising their own messages with the surface forms of male genres, thus managing "the difficult task of achieving true female literary authority by simultaneously conforming to and subverting practical literary standards" (73). This observation may begin to explain why Dickinson chose to gnaw at iambic pentameter mostly from a strict metrical framework in the mid-nineteenth century, rather than radically loosening meter as did her contemporary, Whitman. As a male poet, Whitman could appear to disregard accentual-syllabic prosody, the entire basis of the patriarchal poetic tradition since Chaucer. As a female poet attempting the genre "that has been traditionally the most Satanically assertive, daring, and therefore precarious for women" (Gilbert and Gubar 582), Dickinson could probably not have done so without making her verse impossible—leaving it with no "authority" at all.

Blake and Dickinson looked in the same place for an anti-meter (Hollander's term); Blake's rough fourteeners employ a one-line adaptation of the meter Dickinson favored, the ballad or hymn stanza. The hymn stanza and fourteener carried much less authority than iambic pentameter, being

> rooted, by association, in the poetry which has grown out of the experience of the lower social classes: the ballads of oral tradition, the hymns of the Non-Conformist evangelical revivals, the rhythms of the "Authorized" Bible and of the Psalter. It is, at

once, *the* "common measure" of the tradition, whether it appears in the original long line [alexandrine] or in the . . . ballad-hymn quatrain. (Lewis 129)

In the late eighteenth century, Warton wrote of the seven-foot line that "whatever absolute and original dignity it may boast, at present it is almost ridiculous" (883). Over half a century before Whitman, however, Blake transformed the fourteener pattern into a loose, cadenced accentual meter. Dickinson's choice of the hymn stanza is likely to have been motivated by some of the same concerns that, according to Hollander, may have inspired Blake's choice of the alexandrine: "just as the iambic pentameter had crowded out the late Elizabethan experiments in seven-stressed lines, consigning them to the sub-literary dungeon of doggerel, so Blake may have thought to resurrect them and some of what they stood for" (*Vision* 206). Dickinson treated the anti-meter very differently, staying near, or at least constantly returning to, the strict count of hymn stanzas throughout her career.

In discussing nineteenth-century poetry by women, Gilbert and Gubar note the traditional necessity of self-assertion by the lyric "I" as a central reason for the absence of a great female poet before Dickinson (548). In the nineteenth century "women were still expected to imitate male verse," as Emily Stipes Watts remarks in her history of American female poets (73). But male poets, particularly since Milton, had so objectified women that a female poet writing in the standard meter would adopt "patriarchal plots and genres," an act that "inevitably involves her in duplicity or bad faith" (Gilbert and Gubar 69). The supremely subjective lyric "I"—employed by men for centuries to appropriate the world, the world as woman, and women— seems to have entailed an inversely supreme objectivity in female lyric identity. As a result the most powerful and flexible of English meters, in Louise Bogan's words the "classic and large carrier of English poetry" (210), was not as soon, or as easily, converted and subverted by women as were the male prose genres.

David Porter, in his book on Dickinson's early poetry, notes an ironic component in her use of the hymn stanza:

Inherent in the hymn form is an attitude of faith, humility, and inspiration, and it is against this base of orthodoxy that she so artfully refracts the personal rebellion and individual feeling, the colloquial diction and syntax, the homely image, the scandalous love of this world, and the habitual religious skepticism.[3] (74)

A more hidden irony, reflecting the ambivalence of Dickinson's position as a powerful female poet, can also be seen in her choice of the hymn stanza. Hymns belong to a religious orthodoxy that Dickinson undoubtedly identified as "masculine" (Homans, *Women Writers* 174). By using the meter of the song sung rather than iambic pentameter—the meter of the poet as priest, the traditional singer—Dickinson's poems self-consciously present themselves as harmless "objects." Several feminist critics have discussed the thematic process by which Dickinson adopted idealized, constricting nineteenth-century images of women—the rosy child, the virgin bride—as poetic personae, in effect undermining them from within.[4] In an age full of images of women as angels, the poet's hymn stanza could have had an analogous function. It made the poem an angelic *object* with an original voice, not a singer but a song singing, an implicit comment on the extravagant subjectivity of the pentameter tradition at that time.

After Christina Rossetti's death in 1894, and almost a decade after Dickinson's death, Andrew Lang referred to Rossetti as "the greatest English poet of her sex, which is meant to inspire poetry rather than to create it" (qtd. in Zaturenska 294). Christina Rossetti, like almost all the other "major" recognized English female poets of her day and earlier—Anne Bradstreet, Anne Finch, Aphra Behn, Elizabeth Barrett Browning, and Emily Brontë—wrote a good part of her work in iambic pentameter. Dickinson is the only canonical female poet before the turn of the century who completely resisted the authority of the five-foot iambic line. Her refusal or inability to write it is significantly related, I would argue, to her singular greatness among nineteenth-century female poets. This resistance, however, had negative effects on her reputation that can be traced into our century. On the one hand, the poet J. V. Cunningham, in a short discussion of Dickinson and iambic pentameter, writes that she uses the meter, which occurs in "at most thirty poems," to attain unusual eloquence or simplicity. He guesses that "there was a different and more varied poet, though not necessarily a better one, hidden in the iambic pentameter that never quite got out" (361). On the other hand, John Crowe Ransom completely overlooks Dickinson's pentameters. After noting that the meters Dickinson learned from a household hymnbook limited her because "they excluded all others," he comments that "the great classics of this meter are the English Ballads and Mother Goose" and concludes that

> Folk Line [common meter] is disadvantageous . . . if it denies to the poet the use of English Pentameter when that would be more suitable. Pentameter is the staple of what we may call the studied or "university" poetry, and it is capable of containing and formalizing many kinds of substantive content which would be too complex for Folk Line. Emily Dickinson appears never to have tried it. ("Dickinson's Poetic" 32)

Both poet-critics, whether or not they recognize that Dickinson used iambic pentameter, find that she suffers limitations in complexity or variety for not having used it enough.[5]

Dickinson's occasional choice of iambic pentameter, since the form was entirely alien to her normal practice, was presumably free of the conventional metrical motivations of "establish[ing] a kind of frame around the work as a whole" and signifying, "like a title," how the poem "is to be taken, what sort of thing the poem is to be, and, perhaps . . . what the poet thought he was doing by calling his curious bit of language a poem at all" (Hollander, *Vision* 189). But Dickinson was certainly exposed to the authoritative impact of iambic pentameter: she had a powerful tradition of iambic pentameter behind her, a self-declared ignorance of Whitman ("I never read his book, but was told that it was disgraceful" [*Letters,* no. 254]), and access to a library containing the work of Tennyson, Keats, Robert Browning, Pope, Arnold, Young, Thomson, Shakespeare, William Cullen Bryant, and Elizabeth Barrett Browning, whose portrait she hung on her wall; all of these poets used iambic pentameter.[6]

To the "norm of blank verse" (Hollander, *Vision* 206) Dickinson opposed the hymn stanza, familiar to her through the hymns by Isaac Watts that she had sung in church as a child. Its three standard variations are common meter, in which two lines of four iambic feet alternate with two lines of three iambic feet (4–3–4–3); long meter, in which all the lines have four feet; and short meter, in which only the third line contains four feet (3–3–4–3). Though Porter notes that several of Dickinson's earlier poems "display only a remote connection to regular hymn meters" and employ an irregular mixed meter, even in these poems her lines, with very few exceptions, contain four stresses or fewer (58). In fact, she appears to have scrupulously avoided five-stress lines except, I will argue, where iambic pentameter evokes patriarchal concepts, particularly Christianity and traditional patriarchal poetic and other "author"ity. In the 1,775 poems of the *Complete Poems,* I find 98, including several of her best-known, that use iambic pentameter or an irregular five-stress line—usually only once.[7]

An analysis of Dickinson's iambic pentameters involves determining both the way the words comment on the meter and the relation between the meaning of these lines and that of other lines in the poem. Usually the two aspects of an analysis illuminate one another. Poem 1677 provides a good example:

On my volcano grows the Grass
A meditative spot—
An acre for a Bird to choose
Would be the General thought—

How red the Fire rocks below
How insecure the sod
Did I disclose
Would populate with awe my solitude

The first stanza of this poem presents a place that appears as quiet and unthreatening as does the hymn stanza that describes it. The place is an "acre," a measurable, ownable place, a passive object: the grass grows on it; a bird may choose it. The atmosphere is deceptive, however, and the meter for which this "meditative spot" serves as a figure also conceals unexpected qualities. Though the poetic form of the hymn stanza is not threatening according to "the General thought," the speaker knows that the rocking poetic fire below it is awe inspiring. The iambic pentameter of the poem's final line images the volcano exploding to reveal its power—not surprisingly, since poetic power like that hidden in the first hymn stanza has almost always been embodied in pentameter. The poem makes an unusually clear statement of the sense of confinement and frustration and the threatening tension that accompany the renunciatory poetics of Dickinson's hymn stanza. Rumbling under the surface of the poetic object, the hymn, the ballad, is a subject, a priest, a singer whose isolation could be inhabited (if she "Did [could? wanted to?] disclose") by the authority that "rocks below."

In a discussion of Dickinson's imagery, Joanne Feit Diehl makes an observation that illuminates Dickinson's way of introducing the iambic pentameter line to this poem:

> Dickinson's poems explore ways of combating influence while at the same time allowing the poems to remain open to the influence of the precursor—to maintain the precarious position of receiving his power without being drowned by it. (423)

In poem 1677 the iambic pentameter line, a stand-in for the "precursor," is introduced gradually, through the slow and self-conscious disintegration of the poem's second stanza. The first two lines of this stanza maintain the common meter of the first stanza while describing the precarious balance of the volcano's present state, to which the tactics of the hymn stanza can certainly be compared. The second line—"How insecure the sod"—mentions the insecurity of one arrangement and metrically embodies the insecurity of the other. The metrical aspect of this line's meaning becomes obvious when the following line, the third, is not the four-foot line we would expect in a regular hymn stanza but a two-foot line instead. The two-foot line both metrically and semantically "discloses" that the power rocking below the volcano is capable of explosion: semantically through the subjunctive "Did" and metrically by joining with the second line to form a single "split" iambic pentameter line. The metrical shift is extremely subtle, consisting merely of the rearrangement of the expected four- and three-syllable pattern into a two- and five-syllable pattern. It is emphasized, however, by the syntax of the last three lines: the phrase "Did I disclose" serves as both a syntactic and a metrical hinge, and the final line is a logical unit, complete to the ear as it would not be if the line break followed the word "populate."

When the final, full pentameter line appears in the poem, it has been anticipated, gradually brought to the reader's consciousness, and to some extent forestalled or held off by the split-pentameter tactic. (This pattern is quite common; many of Dickinson's approximately one hundred split pentameters appear in poems that also use full

pentameters.) The metamorphosis from hymn stanza to pentameter
that makes up the second stanza emphasizes that the volcanic explo-
sion is hypothetical and that the poet has complete control over the
pentameter. In the last two lines Dickinson demonstrates that she is
strong enough to hold the line at bay, preventing the poem from
being "drowned," to use Diehl's metaphor, in the awe-inspiring,
solitude-populating majesty of the precursors; and yet the entire
poem is empowered by the tension gained through her simulta-
neously accepting and rejecting their authority.

In "A loss of something ever felt I" (poem 959) a single decasyl-
labic line is similarly postponed until the end of the poem. Here the
metrically ambiguous pentameter is explicitly identified with Christi-
anity rather than with a general "awe" or power:

> A loss of something ever felt I—
> The first that I could recollect
> Bereft I was—of what I knew not
> Too young that any should suspect
>
> A Mourner walked among the children
> I notwithstanding went about
> As one bemoaning a Dominion
> Itself the only Prince cast out—
>
> Elder, Today, a session wiser
> And fainter, too, as Wiseness is—
> I find myself still softly searching
> For my Delinquent Palaces—
>
> And a Suspicion, like a Finger,
> Touches my Forehead now and then
> That I am looking oppositely
> For the site of the Kingdom of Heaven—

The metrical ambivalence evident in this poem's pattern of alter-
nating nine- and eight-syllable lines—the nine-syllable lines coming
within a syllable of pentameters, the eight-syllable lines shrinking
back to the length of regular long hymn-stanza lines—parallels the
ambivalent relationship with Christianity described in the poem.
Both objects of the speaker's ambivalence become clear in the poem's
final line.

A grammatical ambiguity at the end of the second stanza hints
at the ambivalence toward Christianity that will only be made com-

pletely obvious in the poem's final, decasyllabic line: the words "Itself" and "Prince" could refer either to "one"—the "Mourner"—or to the "Dominion" itself. This ambiguity applies to Christianity, as the end of the poem reveals in picking up the Christian connotations of the words "Prince" and "Dominion": insofar as the speaker is seeking and not finding the kingdom of heaven, she feels herself ("Itself") to be "the only Prince cast out"; but insofar as she is "looking oppositely" for it, she is rejecting it, so that the dominion "Itself" is the cast-out prince. An ambiguity is also present in the relation of the poem's final line to iambic pentameter. The ten-syllable line could stand in an iambic pentameter poem; metrically it resembles, for instance, the opening of Shakespeare's sonnet 116, "Let me not to the marriage of true minds." Dickinson's line scans most obviously, however, as three anapests followed by an extra foot. As an iambic pentameter, the line is a deceptive, ambiguous one in which only one syllable—significantly, "King," an unavoidable power over the poem's "Prince"—receives the appropriate metrical stress. Thus iambic pentameter may be seen as an "oppositely" present, "suspected" meaning in the poem, a meaning the poem avoids confronting directly, as it avoids confronting Christian concepts. Both forces are here too strong for any but glancing references. It is not surprising that Christianity and iambic pentameter should receive similar treatment in this Dickinson poem. As Diehl points out, Dickinson's

> precursor is composite, . . . an amalgam of poetic identities . . . which the woman poet identifies with the collective powers of the poetic tradition as well as with the male deity of the Old and New Testaments. . . . The precursor as a composite figure represents to the woman not simply a poet of astonishing authority but the other male personifications of power, the father and God the Father. (423–24)

Like the reference to the "Kingdom of Heaven" in the final line of this poem and the word "awe" in "On my volcano grows the Grass," many of Dickinson's pentameters appear to allude to Christianity in some way. Other examples are "Certificate for Immortality" (poem 1030) and "Even for Death, a fairy medicine" (poem 691). The lines "Itself, too vast, for interrupting—more—" (poem 293) and "Staring—bewildered—at the mocking sky—" (poem 319) might also belong in this list. While not referring specifically to religious power, some pentameters evoke other kinds of potentially oppressive societal forces: "Society for me my misery" (poem 1534); "The Admirations—and Contempts—of time" (poem 906).

In "I rose—because He sank" (poem 616) the pentameter is associated with masculine power in general. It is a rare instance of a pentameter that seems unequivocally to glorify its meter:

> I rose—because He sank—
> I thought it would be opposite—
> But when his power dropped—
> My Soul grew straight.
>
> I cheered my fainting Prince—
> I sang firm—even—Chants—
> I helped his Film—with Hymn—
>
> And when the Dews drew off
> That held his Forehead stiff—
> I met him—
> Balm to Balm—
>
> I told him Best—must pass
> Through this low Arch of Flesh—
> No Casque so brave
> It spurn the Grave—
>
> I told him Worlds I knew
> Where Emperors grew—
> Who recollected us
> If we were true—
>
> And so with Thews of Hymn—
> And Sinew from within—
> And ways I knew not that I knew—till then—
> I lifted Him—

The three split pentameters in this poem set up the penultimate, pentameter line both metrically and thematically. This metrical development parallels the story told in the poem, of gaining power through the weakness of an anonymous male and then using that power to help him—a story with possible Christian undercurrents. The first split pentameter, "But when his power dropped— / My Soul grew straight," uses this meter, which is less authoritative than a full pentameter and which in Dickinson's poems commonly refers to a drop or imperfection in power, to describe the male's loss of power. This drop, while making the meter less authoritative and hence less valuable, also makes it more accessible to the female poet (an implication present in several other of Dickinson's split pentameters—for instance, "We play at Paste— / Till qualified, for Pearl" [poem 320]).[8]

As the poem continues, the combination of two- and three-foot lines describes the comfort the poet brings to the suffering male. It is almost as if the "fainting Prince" she cheers were the authoritative meter itself while the "low Arch" and the "Grave" were figures for the meter's disintegration. The disconnected two- and three-foot lines are finally arranged into two split pentameters in the penultimate stanza, as the comforter nears her goal of lifting "Him." The word "Emperors" suggests the kind of grandeur and patriarchal authority often associated with Dickinson's pentameters, and the mention of a reward gained by being "true" has religious connotations. The word "recollected" also seems to make the self-referential comment that the separated parts of the pentameter are being reunited. In the poem's full pentameter line, "And ways I knew not that I knew—till then—," the speaker seems to become fully conscious of the meter that was only partly obvious in the split pentameters, so that she can derive full strength from it. Ironically, but not surprisingly, this strength is used only to lift "Him": to serve a male principle.

The famous "The Soul selects her own Society" (poem 303) gains strength from the denial of iambic pentameter rather than from its appropriation. Instead of hesitatingly approaching the meter, this poem retreats from its initial iambic pentameter line, a movement that metrically parallels the poem's verbal description of self-reliance and frugality:[9]

> The Soul selects her own Society—
> Then—shuts the Door—
> To her divine Majority—
> Present no more—
>
> Unmoved—she notes the Chariots—pausing—
> At her low Gate—
> Unmoved—an Emperor be kneeling
> Upon her Mat—

I've known her—from an ample nation—
Choose One—
Then—close the Valves of her attention—
Like Stone—

The denial of iambic pentameter in this poem is made vivid by
the description of powerful supplicants, presented in nine-syllable
lines. Like her split pentameters, Dickinson's approximately 130
nine-syllable lines often appear in the same poems as do full iambic
pentameters. In many poems they seem to act as intermediate steps
between the eight-syllable long line of a hymn stanza and the ten-
syllable pentameter line. This poem resists the pentameter to the end
and maintains strong tension by remaining within one syllable of the
pentameter and never settling into a hymn-stanza pattern. Even the
short six-syllable line of the hymn stanza is replaced by two- or
four-syllable lines. The supplicants mentioned in the second stanza
are, both metrically and thematically, authoritative figures humbling
themselves within the boundaries of the hymn stanza. The emperor
kneels and the chariots pause in lines that stop one syllable short of
the imperial English meter, as though these potential pentameters
themselves were "kneeling" and "pausing." The soul rejects the
power of the emperor and the nobility and wealth suggested by the
chariots, just as it rejects the influence and poetic authority carried
by the pentameter.

This poem contains only one pentameter line, the first; having
selected it to be her own "Society"— with all that word connotes—
the soul "shuts the Door" to any further pentameters. Though there
is an "ample nation" of such lines that could be written, the soul has
chosen only "One" of them before closing the "Valves" of her atten-
tion (the valves, in their ability to open and close, resembling the
stresses and releases of metrical feet). Here the poet seems to triumph
in her ability to reject external power and to derive strength from the
little she has chosen to claim as her "own," and the poem might
stand, both in its paradoxical strength and in its dangers, as a meta-
phor for Dickinson's relation to iambic pentameter.

In only one poem does Dickinson appear to be completely over-
come by iambic pentameter. "After great pain, a formal feeling
comes" (poem 341) tries unsuccessfully to resist the fatal stupefaction
of the meter:

After great pain, a formal feeling comes—
The Nerves sit ceremonious, like Tombs—
The stiff Heart questions was it He, that bore,
And Yesterday, or Centuries before?

The Feet, mechanical, go round—
Of Ground, or Air, or Ought—
A Wooden way
Regardless grown
A Quartz contentment, like a stone—

This is the Hour of Lead—
Remembered, if outlived,
As Freezing persons, recollect the Snow—
First—Chill—then Stupor—then the letting go—

The "formal feeling" described in the first line of this poem is embod-
ied metrically in the abundant pentameters. This poem, in fact, con-
tains more pentameters than appear in any other Dickinson poem—
except two (622 and 797), each twice as long. This formal feeling is
presented not positively but, rather, as the aftermath of great pain.
The pain appears to have weakened the poet's resistance to the hyp-
notic, "mechanical," "Wooden way" of the traditional meter.

The words "stiff," "ceremonious," and "Tombs" in the first
stanza's four pentameter lines participate in one complex of concepts
usually associated with Dickinson's pentameters—power, rigidity,
and stasis. The resigned question asked by the stiff heart—"was it
He, that bore?"—seems to refer on one level to Christ's sufferings,
using Christian imagery as Dickinson's pentameters commonly do.
On another level, the question might refer to the burden of subjectiv-
ity and responsibility long borne by male poets, asking whether their
traditional authority should not simply be accepted. In the next
stanza, this poisonous feeling of powerlessness seems to have spread
from the iambic pentameter to iambic feet in general, even those in
two-, three-, or four-foot lines; all such "Feet" are "mechanical" and
move between "Ground" and "Air," stress and unstress, because they
"Ought." The third stanza begins with two lines of common meter,
but the first of these lines scans most readily as a dactylic line. "This
is the Hour of Lead" has the immediacy of self-realization, conveying
the assertive quality characteristic of Dickinson's dactyls. In Dickin-
son's poetry dactyls are much less common than iambic configu-
rations, and they seem to be associated with a relatively powerful

feminine principle contrasted with a masculine force. In poem 945, for example, the soul as a flower, a female figure one assumes from the way it is described in relation to a male, is referred to in dactyls: "Shy as the wind of *his Chambers*" (emphasis added). The end of this poem strongly affirms the importance of this soul: "When it [the flower] is lost, that Day shall be / The Funeral of God." Another example, poem 228, personifies the setting sun as a strong female figure. The account of her activities contains these lines: "Then at the feet of the old Horizon / Laying her spotted Face to die." The first line can be scanned as two dactyls followed by two trochees, but it can also be scanned as iambic pentameter, with the traditional metrical "Horizon" seen as a male force at whose "feet" the female sun dies, insofar as the dactylic meter is eclipsed by the simultaneous pentameter.

In "After great pain," the sudden dactyls are not permeated with the iambic pentameter, but stand out from it; the dactylic movement seems to counteract the lethargy into which the previous stanza's iambs had fallen and to reclaim some integrity for the next iambic hymn-stanza line. Two hymn-stanza lines and two pentameters make up the final stanza of this poem. As the poem ends, the hypothetical phrase "if outlived" leaves the conflict between the two meters open-ended. It is not clear whether the final moment of iambic pentameter stupor will be "outlived." What is clear is that, as the meter of the past poets overtakes the poem, the poet uses iambic pentameter to present an image of helpless, frozen stupor. Lines such as this clearly explain why Dickinson used iambic pentameter as rarely as she did. The meter that seems as if it might empower the poet at the end of "On my volcano grows the grass" has proved itself too strong to be controlled.

As this book will illustrate, numerous lines of free verse can be read fruitfully in terms of the metrical code. This phenomenon should not be astonishing. Writers obviously absorb the regular rhythms of their literature. Quotations of metrical patterns are ready tools for heightened expressiveness, intensity of emotion, assertiveness, or closure. For some free-verse poets, the metrical code adds no more than these to a poem. But for poets like Dickinson who interact intimately with the history of poetic conventions, the metrical code adds a level of profoundly allusive, yet wordless, meaning to poetry.

Chapter 3

Iambic and Dactylic Associations in *Leaves of Grass*

The poetry of Walt Whitman, with Dickinson the other notorious mid-nineteenth-century American rebel against iambic pentameter, might also be expected to show the strength of the meter he opposed, and his loose-limbed poems might be expected not to demonstrate Dickinson's remarkable consistency in metrical attitudes. Both of these suppositions are true. While Whitman's poems engage more deeply with the formal poetic tradition than many critical discussions of his prosody admit, the terms of that engagement do not form nearly as predictable a pattern as they do in Dickinson. Analysis of Dickinson's metrics offers significant evidence of the validity of the theory of the metrical code. Analysis of Whitman's metrics demonstrates the usefulness of the metrical code in illuminating particular passages and tracing analogous attitudes among poems.

An inventory of the iambic pentameter lines in *Leaves of Grass* shows its metrics to be highly sensitive to the power of the canonical meter and as revealing in terms of the metrical code as Dickinson's. Comparative metrical-code readings show that the two poets felt the power of their literary and cultural context in similar ways: both poets associate their iambic pentameters with poetic authority and with the nature of poetry itself, as well as with other powerful inherited cultural traditions such as conventional religion. The differences between their attitudes, often explicable in terms of gender, temperament, and life experience, are equally revealing. Dickinson usually finds the pentameter a suffocating threat to the self—an attitude that correlates with her cultural situation as a female poet. Whitman, by contrast, tends to fall back on the authority of the pentameter as reassurance of the ego's power and autonomy. Both poets associate the pentameter with pain and even imprisonment, but for Whitman such suffering frequently involves the noble demands of war—a theme common in his pentameters and all but absent from Dickinson's.

Although Whitman's iambic pentameters, virtually all of which will be discussed in this chapter, show clearly discernible connotative patterns, the metrical tensions in his poems are less tightly maintained, less structurally crucial, and less consistent than those in Dickinson, and affect his best-known poems less than hers. Not needing to grapple as intimately with the pentameter as did Dickinson, Whitman was free to contribute to a fascinating metrical development that profoundly influenced subsequent American poetry. Whitman explored another whole set of metrical connotations. His poems draw on the metrical-code meanings not only of the iambic pentameter but also of the rhythm I will call, for convenience's sake, dactylic (a term discussed more fully below). Whitman's "dactylic" lines, the large majority of which are also discussed in this chapter, are as consistently connotative as his iambic pentameters.

Whitman's iambic pentameters reveal much about his underlying attitudes toward the poetic past, including attitudes that conflict with his more explicitly stated views. For that reason the iambic pentameters are interesting in themselves. The interactions between the pentameter and the dactylic passages in *Leaves of Grass* also illuminate other aspects of Whitman's poetics. On the metrical no less than on the semantic level, Whitman's poems explore conflicts such as that between the autonomous self and the self merged with others, and between poetry as tradition and poetry as instinctual process. *Leaves of Grass* shows a continual rearrangement of the relations between the iambic pentameter and the dactylic rhythm as it searches over and over for a balance between them and what they represent—a search that Eliot would later continue.

Like Dickinson, Whitman is generally supposed to have forgone the resources of iambic pentameter altogether. But there the similarity ends. Several of Dickinson's critics, as we have seen, assume that her poetry suffers as a result of her metrical choices. Whitman's critics, by contrast, have remained admiring or neutral—if confused—about the metrical character of *Leaves of Grass* since as early as the

1870s. Most of the first reviews in the late 1850s dealt with the problem of the work's singularity, not by criticizing its metric, but by labeling it prose. Hale called it "a sort of prose poetry" (21), Norton "a sort of excited prose broken into lines" (19), and the London *Critic* "innocent of rhythm" (Review of *Leaves of Grass* 42). But by the middle of the next decade, William Dean Howells's judgment that Whitman wrote prose was qualified into the phrase "rhythmic and ecstatic prose" (56). From then on, the growth of Whitman's reputation was accompanied by an increasingly widespread acceptance of his metrical method as authentically poetic, and, eventually, as more and more poetically admirable. By 1878, Dowden admitted the possibility that *Leaves of Grass* might be verse: "Whether we call what he has written verse or prose, . . . it has no copy" (104), and Robert Louis Stevenson accepted it as "rough, unrhymed lyrical verse" (113). The influential Edmund Clarence Stedman referred to it as verse, if "peculiar unrhymed verse," in 1880 ("Review" 116). A *New York Tribune* reviewer summed up the progress of events in 1882: "That he is a poet most of us frankly admit. His merits have been set forth many times" (Review of *Leaves of Grass* 71). Those who thought otherwise were in the minority, however illustrious: in the 1880s, Gerard Manley Hopkins wrote to Robert Bridges that Whitman's work was "mostly in an irregular rhythmic prose" (135), and Swinburne, in his essay "Whitmania," capped an eloquent tirade with the claim that Whitman was as much a poet as was a shoe.[1]

The nineteenth-century ambivalence toward Whitman's metric grew into adulation in the twentieth century. William Carlos Williams wrote of the "freedom with which [Whitman] laid [his verse] on the page" that "it was an order which was essential to the new world" ("Essay" 151). D. H. Lawrence rhapsodized, "The whole soul speaks at once, and is too pure for mechanical assistance of rhyme and measure" (618). Lawrence concludes this claim with a quotation from Whitman in perfectly alternating dactyls and trochees, "out of the cradle endlessly rocking"; although he may have been distinguishing between metrical feet and "mechanical . . . measure," Lawrence may also be as deaf to the metrical regularity of the passage he quotes as Dickinson's critics have tended to be to her pentameters. The acceptance of Whitman's verse as verse has developed so far that his poems have even been criticized for being too metrically regular at times, as Gay Wilson Allen recounts:

> Anyone who examines with care the versification of *Leaves of Grass* will discover many lines that can be scanned with ease, but most critics have regarded such passages as sporadic and uncharacteristic. Several, in fact, have thought the style of "Drum-Taps" inferior to other periods of Whitman's poetry, and a contradiction of his professed theory, because they are much nearer to conventional patterns of verse than his earlier poems. (*New Walt Whitman Handbook* 230)

Thus, while Dickinson has been faulted for not having used the canonical meter, Whitman tends to be praised for abandoning it.

Beyond possible gender stereotyping, there are two likely reasons for this difference in attitude. First, Whitman's own public self-consciousness—the affirmations in his prose writings that he regarded his prosody as revolutionary—give an air of active intentionality to his prosodic experimentation, which no doubt forestalls some criticism. The self-assurance of such statements as "The bases on which all the grand old poems were built have become vacuums" ("Shakespere" 1151) or "The poetic quality is not marshalled in rhyme or uniformity . . . [He] who troubles himself about his ornaments or fluency is lost" (*Leaves of Grass* 716) make criticism of the writer's metrical choices seem like wasted breath. Second, of course, the very thoroughness with which Whitman abandoned metrical regularity makes it harder for modern critics to fault him on his choice of meter than to fault Dickinson. She, after all—no matter how radical her reappropriation of the hymn stanza—remains within the terms of metrical discourse, and presumably open to criticism on metrical grounds.

A thorough discussion of Whitman's pentameters should begin with their place in the metrical texture of the poetry as a whole. Where Dickinson opposes the pentameter almost exclusively with variations on the hymn stanza, the metrical context in which Whitman's pentameters operate is far more elaborate. It consists mostly of dactylic passages, trochaic passages, and fourteeners (a seven-foot iambic line that sounds like half a hymn stanza and often carries exceptionally sentimental or uplifting/religious sentiments in Whitman), as well as many lines in prose rhythms. Of these different rhythms the dactylic passages, though not as frequent as the prose rhythms, are arguably most distinctive and memorable. Many critics have noted the pervasive falling rhythm and the often neatly dactylic lines in *Leaves of Grass,* from Barrett Wendell in his description of Whitman's metric as "hexameters trying to bubble up through sewage" (473) to Paul Elmer More, who maintains that "perfect hexameters abound. . . . The prevailing effect is that of a hexametric cadence such as probably preceded the regular schematisation of the Homeric poems" (243–44), to Edgar Lee Masters, who implies in his persona poem "Petit, the Poet" that Whitman used the same measure as Homer—a measure never named, but instead embodied in the meter of the line that describes it:

> Triolets, villanelles, rondels, rondeaus,
> Seeds in a dry pod, tick, tick, tick,
> Tick, tick, tick, what little iambics,
> While Homer and Whitman roared in the pines?

For every person who asserts the predominance of dactylic lines in Whitman, others point out that the number of true dactylic lines is actually small. But the perception of this rhythm as distinctively Whitmanesque remains, and Whitman's dactyls are an important aspect of his influence on American poets so far.[2]

The use of triple feet, or extra syllables, in iambic verse was a key metrical characteristic of English romantic and later nineteenth-century poetry, marking a separation from the strict syllable counting of eighteenth-century verse in both England and America. To establish the new rhythms against the overwhelming strength of the iambic norm was not a quick or easy process. Paul Fussell notes that it took poets at least 50 years to begin to practice the syllabic freedom first mapped out by prosodic theorists during the 1740s.[3] As late as 1819 in America, William Cullen Bryant published a pleading defense of trisyllabic substitution in verse, concluding with the following description of the still-widespread prejudice against the practice:

> The liberty for which I have been contending, has often been censured and ridiculed. The utmost favour which it has, at any time, to my knowledge, received from the critics, is to have been silently allowed—no one has openly defended it. It has not been my aim to mark its limits or to look for its rules. I have only

attempted to show that it is an ancient birthright of poets, and
ought not to be given up. (431)

Far from being given up, the dactylic rhythm gained acceptance and
popularity in the subsequent few decades. There were Bryant's own
judicious trisyllabic substitutions, the metrical adventures of Poe,
and—finally and incontrovertibly popularizing triple meter as a de-
manding poetic idiom in its own right, not just as a liberty within
iambic meter—the publication of Longfellow's dactylic hexameter
poem *Evangeline* in 1847.[4]

All this dactylic activity set up a metrical alternative to the pre-
vailing iambic meter, a counterforce whose connotative power would
eventually become almost as alluring as that of iambic pentameter to
a significant number of metrically variable American poets. Dickin-
son's metrics evidence the roots of this situation; I have mentioned
the unusual associations with female strength and clarity of percep-
tion that Dickinson's handful of dactylic rhythms convey (see pages
29–30). But the unique counterbalance that enabled Dickinson to
explore and resist the canonical meter in metrically variable verse
well before any other American poet except Whitman was the hymn
stanza, not the triple foot. Triple feet are not essential to Dickinson's
freedom from pentameter, as they proved to be for other American
poets.

For American poets in general, Longfellow's hexameters and
Whitman's triple rhythms were crucial in establishing a new freedom
of resources, an enlarged metrical vocabulary. Remarkably quickly,
the "new" metrical mode came to carry a connotative weight capable
of balancing the four centuries of iambic pentameter's hegemony.
On the surface, Whitman's exploration of both dactylic and pentame-
ter connotations in *Leaves of Grass*—which put both rhythms side by
side in a free verse matrix—may seem singlehandedly to have lent the
dactylic rhythm a semantic force equivalent to that of the iambic
pentameter.

But, of course, several factors in the prosodic climate of the
nineteenth century (including the revived interest in classical meters,
which will be discussed in the next chapter) allowed Whitman and his
free-verse successors to find so much meaning in triple rhythms. One
explanation for the speed with which the triple meter acquired its
special force can be derived from Martin Halpern's influential 1962

article "On the Two Chief Metrical Modes in English." Halpern proposes that there are really only two kinds of meter in English verse: iambic meter, and everything else. According to Halpern, a trochaic poem like "Hiawatha" and a dactylic poem like *Evangeline* are closely associated metrically, since both of their meters tend to fall into patterns of absolute stress and unstress, as opposed to the many gradations of stress possible in iambic lines. Halpern posits that anapestic, trochaic, and dactylic rhythms—all of which he sees as isochronic and isoaccentual—are alike "simply variants" of the native Anglo-Saxon strong-stress rhythm (177). This idea would explain the influence of triple rhythms in the nineteenth and twentieth centuries by their appeal to a powerful innate capacity of the English language or the English-speaking ear. Edward Weissmuller corroborates this possiblity when he notes the preponderance of triple-foot-like patterns in Anglo-Saxon verse and describes the nineteenth-century establishment of triple feet as a situation in which

> irreducible triple rhythms from one side of our poetic heritage... invaded the artificially and precariously maintained duple rhythms we learned so thoroughly and so long ago from Romance syllabic verse... that duple rhythm became a rival heritage, its artificiality for centuries as natural to us somehow as the cheerful, returning thump of a nursery rhyme. (287)

One obvious problem with the idea that triple meters had the appeal of the strong-stress tradition, however, is that Whitman and other free-verse poets do not, in practice, usually write in regular strong-stress meter any more than they write in strict triple meter. Sculley Bradley has made an interesting case for Whitman as a strong-stress prosodist. He analyzes certain passages of the poetry in terms of a "hovering accent" that gives stress value to word groups of widely varying lengths. Most writers agree with Roger Mitchell, however, that Whitman's poetry is far too irregularly stressed for such a method to be systematically applied (1606).

Edwin Fussell appeals to the American quest for national identity, rather than to any characteristic of the English language itself, to explain the ease with which dactylic rhythm established itself in the American poetic ear:

> Used sparingly, flexibly and with genuine delicacy, as Whitman
> so often uses it, falling rhythm is undeniably one of the most
> rewarding metrical maneuvers for the American poet. Simply
> because it strikes the ear—even the American ear—as unusual, it
> immediately frees [the American poet] from his nervous appre-
> hension of being overwhelmed by English lilt. (42)

This idea does not account for the simultaneous appeal of such meters
to poets such as Arnold, Robert Browning, Scott, and Tennyson in
nineteenth-century Great Britain; on the other hand, however, the
hypothesis that triple feet and falling rhythms are more integral to
American than to British poetry could explain the more dramatic
flourishing of free verse in America later (see the discussion of the
relation between triple rhythms and free verse on pp. 65–66). An
even simpler explanation of the triple-foot phenomenon on both con-
tinents, however, is that the triple rhythm was simply a natural next
step after the iamb had worn itself out by exhaustive use.[5]

Whatever the inadequacies of each of these explanations of nine-
teenth-century metrical developments, in combination they some-
what demystify the ease with which dactylic rhythms acquired
significance for the American poetic ear—and hence the applicability
of the metrical code to dactylic passages as well as to iambic pentame-
ter. Once the authority of *Leaves of Grass,* not to mention Longfel-
low's poems in triple meters, had been firmly established towards the
end of the nineteenth century, the evocative semantic power of the
dactyl becomes evident in the free verse of poets like Stephen Crane
and Eliot. It is hard, however, to imagine any of this having hap-
pened without Whitman.

Whitman was not the first to use dactylic rhythms in America
or in England. Nor was he even the first to use his own combination
of various metrical and prose rhythms. Bliss Perry points out the
close similarity between Whitman's prosody and that in Samuel War-
ren's 1851 poem "The Lily and the Bee" (95–96), and others, includ-
ing Timothy Steele, note the stylistic similarity between Whitman
and Martin Tupper (198). But Whitman's extensive exploration of
the connotative pull of the dactyl seems to have been original in
American poetry. Whitman treats the dactyl very differently than
Dickinson does the hymn stanza. Each poet uses the less orthodox
meter as a foil or opposition to iambic pentameter, but Whitman's

dactyls—actually fewer in number than his pentameters—are as charged with associations for him as the more established meter. Dickinson's hymn stanza, although it sometimes carries a self-conscious meaning, most often acts as a kind of neutral metrical ground from which she can approach the pentameter.[6] Whitman's prose rhythms usually take on this neutral role, leaving his dactyls free to convey their own cloud of meanings.

The two very first lines of *Leaves of Grass,* the opening of the initial prefatory "Inscription," set up a metrical and ideological opposition between the pentameter and the dactylic line that persists throughout the book. The two meters pull actively against each other on the semantic level:

> One's-Self I sing, a simple separate person,
> Yet utter the word Democratic, the word En-Masse.

The individual self, with emphasis on its "separate"-ness, here appears balanced in tension against the mass, the democratic group, in whose identity an individual might become lost. The iambic pentameter, a line that Whitman consistently uses to glorify the power of independent individuality, presents this separate self. The iambic pentameter performs the same function in the first line of "Song of Myself," "I celebrate myself, and sing myself," and in line 10 of "A Song for Occupations," "Neither a servant nor a master I." The second line of the passage is almost perfectly dactylic, with an initial hypermetrical syllable that echoes the final hypermetrical syllable of the pentameter. This line could also—and perhaps even more properly—be scanned as iambs and anapests. My choice to scan it as, and call it, dactylic—here and in other such cases—is not a judgment on the best way of scanning the line. I use the word *dactylic* as a sign for the rhythmic similarity and the semantic kinship between such lines and the many technically dactylic lines in Whitman. Dactylic here signifies a characteristic and recognizable rhythmic tendency consisting predominantly of falling rhythms and triple feet, although Whitman's primarily dactylic lines also occasionally include duple feet, a possibility included in the traditional term *dactylic line.* While the lines that I will call Whitman's dactylic lines do not all scan alike—particularly those that, like the line under discussion, begin with an unstressed syllable—they share a distinctive sound pattern and refer to a closely related cluster of semantic associations. The term *dactylic,* as opposed to *triple meter,* also evokes the cultural legacy of the classical dactylic hexameter, which seems to play no small part in Whitman's sense of the meter.

The dactylic line and the iambic pentameter in this initial couplet logically oppose each other, a relationship signaled by the word "yet." The dactylic line evokes a group of connotations—group identity and communion with others—consistent with the general set of meanings in Whitman's dactyls; other, roughly related, meanings are darkness and invisibility, bodily knowledge and intuition as opposed to rational knowledge, and freedom from traditional conventions. Whitman's dactylic lines usually refer to looser clusters of meaning than his iambic pentameters, which evoke their connotations more straightforwardly. The line under discussion, however, connects to the democractic theme of other dactylic lines in *Leaves of Grass* with specific words: a line in "Song of Myself: "I speak the pass-word primeval, I give the sign of democracy," and one in "Years of the Modern": "Is there going to be but one heart to the globe? Is humanity forming en masse?"[7]

The conjunction between the individual self celebrated in iambic pentameter and the group identity evoked in the dactylic line connects to a central point of tension in Whitman. Roy Harvey Pearce describes a characteristic movement in Whitman's poetry as follows:

> In Whitman's poetry, the ego is made not only to assert but to preserve itself. Its tremendous creative powers somehow militate against that fusion of ego and cosmos . . . which seems to have been a major need of the late Whitman. (166)

The connotations of Whitman's dactyls verge on loss of self; the rhythm for him embodies a "fusion of ego and cosmos" that stimulates his threatened ego to respond, on occasion, with an assertion of poetic selfhood in the form of a reliable, traditional iambic pentameter. In "Quicksand Years," for instance, a final iambic pentameter shores up the speaker's ego against the preceding barrage of dactylic lines evoking chaos and mutability:

> Quicksand years that whirl me I know not whither,
> Your schemes, politics, fail, lines give way,

substances mock and elude me,
Only the theme I sing, the great and strong-
    possess'd soul, eludes not,
One's-self must never give way—that is the final
    substance—that out of all is sure,
Out of politics, triumphs, battles, life, what at
    last finally remains?
When shows break up what but One's-Self is sure?

The dactylic lines describe the mystery and the horror of a loss of self; metrically they evoke the horror of a loss of poetic authority. At the beginnings of lines 3 and 4, the poet affirms the value of the self in iambic rhythms, trying to establish its worth on both the semantic and the metrical levels. As each of these lines falls back into a falling rhythm, he proves more successful on the semantic than on the metrical level. Perhaps due to that failure, the penultimate, dactylic line remains in the form of a question, not clearly a rhetorical one. The recurrence of "politics" twice in this poem chimes with "democracy" and "en-masse" in dactylic lines elsewhere in Whitman, although here the concept of politics participates in the sense of all human endeavor as "shows" of shadowy, shifting phenomena. Only with the iambic pentameter line, a truly rhetorical question, can the poet maintain the reassuring presence of the self to his own satisfaction—a resolution that seems to allow his poem to end.

The defensive nature of the iambic pentameter–embodied self threatened by dactylic shapelessness is clear in a line from "Autumn Rivulets," one of those few and fascinating single lines in which the dactylic and iambic rhythms with their attendant connotations co-exist and even overlap. Here the resolute and unequivocal self-reliance of the self plays its part again: "The soul has that measureless pride which revolts from every lesson but its own." At the word "every," suddenly the line cannot be scanned in triple feet any longer. The mystical, seamless state of communion that has been evoked by the term "measureless" is brought up short by one unexpected stress, which pulls forward an even more familiar metrical pattern—the iambic pentameter. One must backtrack to the beginning of the word "revolts" and read again in order to make metrical sense of the rest of the line, a textbook iambic pentameter asserting the complete self-reliance and clear boundaries of the soul.

At times, Whitman's iambic pentameters reveal an implicit rather

than an explicitly represented self. The self appears as self-conscious-
ness, an awareness of the self in opposition to direct, unmediated
experience, in "Good-bye My Fancy!":

> Now for my last—let me look back a moment;
> The slower fainter ticking of the clock is in me.
> Exit, nightfall, and soon the heart-thud stopping.

The poet contemplates death in the pentameter (the first line), but
represents death as direct experience in a falling rhythm (the third
line). In transition between the two, the second line begins with a
regular pentameter and then drifts off into uncertainty with the addi-
tional words "is in me"—as if the realization of the actual immediacy
of death made it impossible to sustain the removed perspective of the
pentameter any longer.

While many of the iambic pentameters asserting the self in
Whitman can be analyzed as a metrical and semantic response to the
pressure of dactylic rhythms, others occur independently of any par-
ticular metrical context. Of these pentameters, a large number have
to do with poetry itself, almost as if the semantic context, the theme
of poetry, were triggering the same defensive response sometimes
brought on by a metrical context, the flow of dactyls. In each case,
the iambic pentameter serves as a recourse to a traditional poetic
persona.

This "poetic" aspect of the metrical code in Whitman is particu-
larly evident in those lines I call his *metapentameters*. Often occurring
at the beginnings, and sometimes at the ends, of poems, these pen-
tameters provide a culturally sanctioned poetic jumping-off place for
the less metrical lines. The opening of the first inscription discussed
above is such a pentameter. So is the first line of "Song of Myself,"
which Whitman augmented, in the process of revision, to make the
1855 line "I celebrate myself" into a full iambic pentameter. As Albert
Gelpi has remarked, "The second phrase contributes little to the
thought of the line, but it makes explicit the epic intentions in . . . the
line associated since Milton with epic in English" (169). Initial meta-
pentameters also occur in various of Whitman's "occasional" poems
that engage in conventional nineteenth-century poetic addresses, such
as "Outlines for a Tomb," an elegy for philanthropist George

Peabody, which opens, "What may we chant, O thou within this tomb?" or "To Those Who've Failed" (originally titled "A Laurel Wreath to Those Who've Failed"), which opens, "To those who've failed, in aspiration vast . . ."

Whitman's initial pentameters respond not only to such conventional themes; the simple occasion of opening a poem often suffices to inspire a metapentameter. Among the 396 separate poems of *Leaves of Grass*, over 15 percent (61 poems) begin with scannable iambic pentameters. In an additional 27 poems, for example "Passage to India," which opens "Singing my days, / Singing the great achievements of the present," the second line is a pentameter. 24 further poems have the line I call an *embedded iambic pentameter*—a scannable pentameter forming the beginning or end of a longer line—as the first or second line. An example is the first line of "O Magnet-South": "O magnet-South! O glistening perfumed South—my South!," where a pentameter with one trisyllabic substitution in the fourth foot constitutes the portion of the line before the dash. Thus, an iambic pentameter appears in the first two lines of 112 poems, well over a quarter of all the poems in *Leaves of Grass*.

The apparent sense of the poem itself as a "poetic" occasion extends to the last lines of many of Whitman's poems as well. Barbara Herrnstein Smith has remarked, "One of the most significant ways in which form contributes to our sense of the integrity of a poem is by, in effect, drawing an enclosing line around it" (25). The enclosing metapentameter that marks many of Whitman's poems as poems does so at the end as well as at the beginning. In "When I Heard the Learn'd Astronomer," for instance, a profusion of different metrical patterns finally concludes in one perfectly regular pentameter:

When I heard the learn'd astronomer,
When the proofs, the figures, were ranged in columns before me,
When I was shown the charts and diagrams, to add, divide, and
    measure them,
When I sitting heard the astronomer where he lectured with much
    applause in the lecture-room,
How soon unaccountable I became tired and sick,
Till rising and gliding out I wander'd off by myself,
In the mystical moist night-air, and from time to time,
Look'd up in perfect silence at the stars.

The line lengths and rhythms in this poem as a whole are very ir-
regular, even for Whitman, but it is framed by an initial headless
iambic pentameter and a final pentameter that provides a strong
sense of closure. The last line furnishes a balanced regular pattern of
stresses to rest the reader's ear, and it brings the rough five-stress
pattern of the preceding three lines to a satisfying prominence. Per-
haps most importantly, however, the last line draws on the com-
mon perception of the pentameter as a "poetic" rhythm. It provides
closure by laying to rest anxieties over the nature of this text that
may have been raised by the irregularities of the rest of the poem.
The image of the very speaker who has just uttered this rather
wordy poem regarding the stars "in perfect silence" adds another
element of surrender to the poem's metrical surrender to the pen-
tameter tradition. *Leaves of Grass* as a whole is also enclosed by
metapentameters; the final edition not only begins with an iambic
pentameter, quoted above; it ends with one as well: "the modern
world to thee and thought of thee!"

While the subjects of the poems with initial or closing metapen-
tameters seem to run the gamut of Whitman's themes, there is one
commonality: more of these lines occur in the later poems than in the
earlier work. William Thayer, in his memoir of Whitman, quotes the
elderly poet as saying,

> Nobody could write in my way unless he had a melody singing
> in his ears. I don't always contrive to catch the best musical
> combination nowadays; but in the older pieces I always had a
> tune before I began to write. (488)

The pentameters may have been more likely to move into a Whitman
poem in the absence of another definite "tune." Ideological factors
may have been contributing to an increase of metapentameters in the
later Whitman as well. Whitman remarks in "Poetry Today in Amer-
ica":

> Years ago I thought Americans ought to strike out separate, and
> have expressions of their own in highest literature. I think so still,
> and more decidedly than ever. But those convictions are now
> strongly temper'd by some additional points, (perhaps the result
> of advancing age, or the reflections of invalidism). I see that this

world of the West, as part of all, fuses inseparably with the East, and with all, as time does. . . . If we are not to hospitably receive and complete the inaugurations of the old civilizations, and change their small scale to the largest, broadest scale, what on earth are we for? . . . what has been fifty centuries growing, working in, and accepted as crowns and apices for our kind, is not going to be pulled down and discarded in a hurry. (*Specimen Days* 291–92)

Whitman uses initial and final metapentameters more in response to context (the expectations brought to a poem qua poem) than to content. But his metapentameters do not respond only to his poems' own literary self-assertions—the implicit claim that a text is *being* a poem as it begins and ends.[8] Many other metapentameters connect closely to the poems' content, reacting to, or participating in, the evocation of the theme of "poetry" within a poem. The pentameters in the following lines set up an implicit standard for the poetic situation described, as if metrically they evoke "true" or "inmost" poetry: "The words of true poems do not merely please" ("Song of the Answerer"); "to penetrate the inmost lore of poets" ("To Get the Final Lilt of Songs"). In "To a Locomotive in Winter," the Muse serves a similar function, standing in as a synecdoche for the poetic standard in an embedded pentameter: "For once come serve the Muse and merge in verse." The metrical/semantic message of such lines contrasts startlingly with the explicit rejection of traditional definitions and forms of poetry in Whitman's writings.

The iambic pentameter functions similarly, and the Muse appears at greater length, in the long occasional poem "Song of the Exposition," a poem with one of the highest concentrations of iambic pentameters in *Leaves of Grass*. Whitman invites the Muse first to migrate from the Old World in an iambic pentameter—to make her feel at home in proper verse, it seems: "Come Muse migrate from Greece and Ionia." (The fact that the pentameter here is intended to reassure the Muse that American civilization is not entirely barbaric is supported later in the poem, when he entreats her to "Fear not O Muse! . . . [here are] / the same old love, beauty and use the same.") Almost immediately after inviting the Muse to migrate, the poet slips into a rejection of ancient culture, in the appropriated classical dactylic rhythm:

Cross out please those immensely overpaid accounts,
That matter of Troy and Achilles' wrath, and
    Aeneas', Odysseus' wanderings,
Placard "removed" and "To Let" on the rocks of your
    snowy Parnassus . . .

The last line above, a regular dactylic hexameter, uses the Muse's ancient meter to urge her out of old haunts and into the modern environment of America, whose technological triumphs Whitman sanctifies with the pentameter in "Song of the Exposition" ("with lines of steamships threading every sea") and elsewhere, for example in the line "I see the tracks of the railroads of the earth" ("Salut Au Monde"). After the Muse has accepted his offer and arrives here, a subsequent passage continues to contrast the Muse's presence here, in an iambic pentameter (the first line below), with dactylic descriptions of all she is leaving behind:

She comes! I hear the rustling of her gown . . .
Silent the broken-lipp'd Sphinx in Egypt, silent all those century-
    baffling tombs,
Ended for aye the epics of Asia's, Europe's helmeted warriors, ended
    the primitive call of the muses,
Calliope's call forever closed, Clio, Melpomene, Thalia dead,
Ended the stately rhythmus of Una and Oriana, ended the quest of the
    holy Graal . . .

The metrical opposition at this point in the poem implies that America's claim to the Muse rests on our Western European antecedents, another idea that contrasts with most of Whitman's explicit statements about American poetry. Associations between the pentameter and traditional European culture abound in Whitman. Some representative lines are: "I hear continual echoes from the Thames" ("Salut Au Monde"); "And royal feudal Europe sails with thee" and "By you and all your teeming life old Thames" ("Outlines for a Tomb"); "More picturesque than Rhenish castle keeps" ("Song of the Exposition"); "Bring the old pageants, show the feudal world" ("The Mystic Trumpeter"). The association of dactylic rhythms with exotic and ancient cultures appears elsewhere in *Leaves of Grass* as well, notably in "Passage to India":

Nor you alone ye facts of modern science,
But myths and fables of eld, Asia's, Africa's fables,
The far-darting beams of the spirit, the unloos'd dreams,
The deep-diving bibles and legends,
The daring plots of the poets, the elder religions;
O you temples fairer than lilies . . .

In this passage, the ancient, Eastern civilizations described in the dactylic rhythms contrast with the Western and modern world described in the initial pentameter, as they do in the Muse passages of "Song of the Exposition."

Later in "Song of the Exposition," however, Whitman attempts to reconcile the two cultural and metrical forces. At the end of section 3, the Muse makes her way through a metrical hodgepodge and ensconces herself triumphantly, in an iambic pentameter, in modern America:

Making directly for this rendezvous, vigorously
clearing a path for herself, striding through the confusion,
By thud of machinery and shrill steam-whistle undismay'd,
Bluff'd not a bit by drain-pipe, gasometers, artificial fertilizers,
She's here, install'd amid the kitchen ware!

Whitman is not content to leave her there. His ideal Muse will not confine herself to the pentameter; he feels she should bring her ancient meters along with her. In one of the most interesting moments of the poem on a metrical-code level, Whitman describes to the Muse, in rough but increasingly dactylic rhythms, the catalog of American wonders she can now begin to sing:

You shall see the crude ores of California and Nevada passing on and
    on till they become bullion,
You shall watch how the printer sets type, and learn what a composing-
    stick is,
You shall mark in amazement the Hoe press whirling its cylinders,
    shedding the printed leaves steady and fast,
The photograph, model, watch, pin, nail shall be created before you.

This is a poignant passage. The pentameter is still the metapoetic line, the line that has endowed the poet with the authority to invite the Muse to America, the line that has brought the "rustling of her

gown" and installed her "among the kitchen ware." Even in the final
sections of the poem, Whitman relies on the pentameter to endow his
formal declarations to the Muse with the power of performative ut-
terances: "I say I bring thee Muse today and here, / All occupations,
duties broad and close . . . We dedicate, dread Mother, all to thee!"
But he uses the meter of "snowy Parnassus," the rhythm of the
"broken-lipp'd Sphinx," to show the Muse the putatively epic won-
ders of the New World. The content of the lines is straightforward
and confident, but the meter adds another dimension: an entreaty
that she will find these industrial wonders worthy of the dignity of
her ancient meter and bless America with her accustomed poetry.

However profound Whitman's connection with, and veneration
for, triple measures, the iambic pentameter remains the meter of his
own poetic tradition and his own consciousness of "writing poetry."
A passage like the following, from "Thanks in Old Age," clearly
links the pentameter with the knowledge that the poet is writing a
book that is like other books, and will have readers:

> You distant, dim unknown—or young or old—countless, unspecified,
>   readers belov'd,
> We never met, and ne'er shall meet—and yet our souls embrace, long,
>   close, and long.

The first of these two lines consists entirely of two embedded pen-
tameters, which evoke literary tradition in the form of the readers of
the future. In the second line the poet reassures himself, in the embed-
ded pentameter after the dash, that he is a part of the literary tradition
and that therefore his book will be comprehensible to these unmet
future readers. A similar consciousness of writing a book for readers
appears in the following pentameter from "As Consequent, Etc.,"
"In you whoe'er you are my book perusing," while the act of creating
poetry itself evokes the pentameter in the first line of "As I Sit Writ-
ing Here," "As I sit writing here, sick and grown old," and the last
line of "Then Last of All": "The brain that shapes, the voice that
chants this song." In "Thou Mother With Thy Equal Brood," the
poet addresses the nation self-consciously in the pentameter metrical
"formula": "But greater still from what is yet to come, / Out of that
formula for thee I sing." A line beginning a discussion of the ideal
poet in "Song of the Answerer," "The indications and tally of time,"

uncannily resembles a pentameter in Dickinson's poem 906: "The Admirations—and Contempts—of time." Both lines explain their own metricality by implying the poets' awareness of future reactions to their work.

Another group of pentameters in *Leaves of Grass*, while not always referring explicitly to literature, uses the meter to celebrate the value of traditional life and the importance of many kinds of conventional virtues. Such themes include cleanliness: "That all is clean forever and forever" ("This Compost"); community: "Or sit at table at dinner with the rest" ("Miracles"); religion: "I see religious dances old and new" ("Proud Music of the Storm"); and daily labor: "The countless workmen working in the shops" ("Our Old Feuillage"). Another sizable group of pentameters celebrates tranquil, cultivated prosperity, for example in the lines: "Sat peaceful parents with contented sons" ("Outlines for a Tomb") and "Thou lucky Mistress of the tranquil barns" ("The Return of the Heroes").

But there is a flip side to these fruitful limitations. In "Song of the Universal," the pentameter line evincing faith in a meaningful universal order contrasts gratefully with the nonpentameter lines that surround it: "O the blest eyes, the happy hearts, / that see, that know the guiding thread so fine / along the mighty labyrinth." But in "To a Foil'd European Revoutionaire," the pentameter line invoking political loyalty is rejected by the following line: "Not songs of loyalty alone are these / but songs of insurrection also." In "Song of Myself," the power of the pentameter itself is appropriated for anarchistic purposes quite opposite to its more usual meaning in Whitman: "No guard can shut me up, no law prevent me."

These negative pentameter connotations are not surprising. Not only does the metrical code reveal how deeply Whitman felt the power and value of the iambic pentameter tradition; it helps to explain his revolt against it. Like Dickinson, even if less passionately and desperately, Whitman was ambivalent about a meter that conveyed both authority and oppression. One group of pentameters, for instance, conveys a sense of decayed aristocracy that is perfectly congruent with Whitman's description of "British Literature" as "cold, anti-democratic, loves to be sluggish and stately" (*Specimen Days* 325). Using the meter of British poetic tradition, Whitman evokes images such as "The noble sire fallen on evil days" ("Virginia—The West"), a former queen "now lean and tatter'd seated on the ground"

("Old Ireland"), and "The sack of an old city in its time" ("Song of the Broad-Ax").

Many other of Whitman's pentameters involve images of war and pain. The number of metrical lines in "Drum-Taps" has been noted by several critics. Gay Wilson Allen observes:

> Apparently the poet found more conventional metrics either convenient or necessary for the expression of his experiences and emotions connected with the war. Even "Pioneers! O Pioneers!" is a marching poem. But what is more natural than that the poet's heartbeat would throb to the rhythms of marching feet—especially a poet who aspired to give organic expression to his own age and country? (*New Walt Whitman Handbook* 241–42)

Not only in "Drum-Taps" but throughout *Leaves of Grass,* pentameters express sentiments such as "To see men fall and die and not complain!" ("A Song of Joys"), "I hear the great shells shrieking as they pass" ("The Artilleryman's Vision"), and "And Death, defeat, and sisters', mothers' tears" ("The Centenarian's Story"). Allen's connection between regular metrics and marching rhythms does much to explain the preponderance of this type of pentameter in Whitman. But the fact that many other pentameters in *Leaves of Grass* express pain and suffering having nothing to do with war suggests that other factors may be at work here as well.

Pentameters that express imprisonment, such as "Inside these breast-bones I lie smutch'd and choked" ("You Felons on Trial in Courts") or defeat, such as "O baffled, balk'd, bent to the very earth" ("As I Ebb'd With the Ocean of Life") bring to mind the Dickinson line, "First—Chill—then Stupor—then the letting go" (poem 341). The preponderence of such images in iambic pentameter as opposed to dactylic lines in Whitman suggests that, like Dickinson, Whitman felt the pentameter itself as at times stifling and painful. Other iambic pentameter descriptions of pain in Whitman are even more dramatic, such as "The livid cancer spread its hideous claws" ("Thou Mother with Thy Equal Brood") or "And feel the dull unintermitted pain" ("Song of Myself"). In the face of such lines, the frequency with which Whitman used the pentameter testifies to the strength of its pull on him.

But, as I have discussed elsewhere, Whitman wanted the Muse

to sing in dactyls; he had other options besides iambic pentameter. In some of the most interesting lines, prosodically, in *Leaves of Grass*, on the metrical-code level metapentameters and metadactyls represent ideas of poetry that contrast with each other. An example is the final passage of "Lo, Victress on the Peaks":

> No poem proud, I chanting bring to thee, nor mastery's rapturous
>   verse,
> But a cluster containing night's darkness and blood-dripping wounds,
> And psalms of the dead.

An embedded iambic pentameter, with a caesura after the second foot, begins the first line. This embedded pentameter performs the triple function of embodying the canonical meter, describing the confidence and strength of its own metrical tradition, and rejecting that tradition. The triple feet in the second part of the line reject the "rapturous" dactylic rhythm as well, but only to pick it up at even greater length in the second line, which evokes the vagueness, darkness, and mysterious power typical in Whitman's dactylic lines. A similar dialectic appears in "Song of the Answerer":

> The words of true poems do not merely please . . .
> The words of the true poems give you more than poems . . .
> They prepare for death, yet they are not the finish, but rather the outset,
> They bring none to his or her terminus or to be content and full,
> Whom they take they take into space to behold the birth of stars, to
>   learn one of the meanings,
> To launch off with absolute faith, to sweep through the ceaseless rings
>   and never be quiet again.

The word *poem* appears in each of the pentameters, the first two lines quoted—just as it did in the embedded pentameter discussed above. Like many other of Whitman's metapentameters, these two use the power of the traditional meter to evoke a culturally sanctioned sense of "poetry." But, unlike the majority of his metapentameters, these evoke the power only for it to be rejected. A more sublime and indescribable power appears in the triple meters to displace the tame literariness described in the pentameters. As if to underscore the otherworldly quality of the new meter and of the experience described, the falling rhythm comes into its full power at the phrase "take into

space," and pushes off most strongly of all at "launch off with abso-
lute faith."

At times the ineffable quality of Whitman's dactyls extends to a
rejection, not only of poems, but of words themselves. This phe-
nomenon appears in miniature in this line from "Shut Not Your
Doors," which slips into a dactylic rhythm with the word "drift":
"The words of my book nothing, the drift of it everything." The
final two dactyls in this line offer an alternative to the words that the
first part of the line has rejected. The third section of "A Song of the
Rolling Earth" makes the same metrical point on a larger scale, with
rough but persistent dactylic rhythms rejecting the value of words:

> I swear I begin to see little or nothing in audible words,
> All merges toward the presentation of the unspoken meanings of the
>   earth,
> Toward him who sings the songs of the body and of the truths of the
>   earth,
> Toward him who makes the dictionaries of words that print cannot
>   touch.

In these examples, the power of dactylic rhythms to connote
meanings beyond the scope of words is supreme. But occasionally,
the dialectic has a different outcome. The pentameter's power to
articulate culturally accepted speech is sometimes cause for celebra-
tion and gladness, as in the line, "A swift and swelling ship full of
rich words," the last line of "A Song of Joys." And sometimes, the
ineffability of dactyls compared to the pentameter is a limitation. In
"Who Learns My Lesson Complete?" the poet equates dactylic
speechlessness not with transcendence, but with infancy: "And pass'd
from a babe in the creeping trance of a couple of summers and winters
to articulate and walk." The phrase "pass'd from a babe in the creep-
ing trance of a couple of summers" forms a classical dactylic hexame-
ter; the rest of the line switches seasons and grows into adulthood in
an iambic pentameter.

The connotations of Whitman's iambic pentameters and of his
dactylic rhythms are often at odds, whether they oppose constraint
to freedom, strength of self to loss of self, Europe to Asia, the mod-
ern to the ancient, or reason to intuition. At certain moments in
Leaves of Grass, however, the two meters harmonize and even coop-
erate in the service of a poem. Such a moment occurs in "Warble for

Lilac-Time." The poem opens with an appeal from the poet to his soul, beginning with two lines that include embedded pentameters:

> Warble me now for joy of lilac-time, (returning in reminiscence,)
> Sort me O tongue and lips for Nature's sake, souvenirs of earliest summer.

In the two initial, imperative clauses, the pentameter voices a sort of epic invocation to inspire the soul to produce poetry. But this very appeal becomes the poem itself as the speaker, using a combination of different meters, describes what the soul should include in the poem. Two contiguous meters, for instance—a pentameter and a primarily dactylic line—fuse harmoniously in the description of the robin: "the robin where he hops, bright-eyed, brown-breasted, / With musical clear call at sunrise, and again at sunset . . ." When the speaker addresses the soul again, dactylic lines replace the pentameter: "come, let us lag here no longer, let us be up and away! / O if one could but fly like a bird." The dactylic rhythms suit this appeal for freedom, just as the pentameter suits the initial appeal to the soul to make poetry. Dactylic lines connote many kinds of freedoms in Whitman's poems, and they explicitly refer to escape in lines such as "Out of the dark confinement! Out from behind the screen!" ("Song of the Open Road"). In "Warble for Lilac-Time" the poet uses each meter for different purposes as he addresses his own soul. The pentameter and the dactylic line each invoke their own specific connotations, and the contrast accomplishes one common rhetorical goal.

In a passage from "Old Chants," a fanciful vignette depicts such a harmony between the two meters allegorically. The poet is addressing the "Mother of All":

> Musing, seeking themes fitted for thee,
> *Accept for me,* thou saidst, *the elder ballads,*
> *And name for me before thou goest each ancient poet.*

The poet, acknowledging the New World's debt "to old poems," recites a catalog of world literature from ancient Egypt to Victorian England. The poem concludes with a description of the interaction between all these poets and the Mother of All:

As some vast wondrous weird dream-presences,
the great shadowy groups gathering around,
Darting their mighty masterful eyes forward at thee,
Thou! with as now thy bending neck and head, with courteous hand
    and word, ascending,
Thou! pausing a moment, drooping thine eyes upon them, blent with
    their music,
Well pleased, accepting all, curiously prepared for by them,
Thou enterest at thy entrance porch.

The poem as a whole has been almost entirely in prose rhythms, but
at the climactic interaction between literary tradition and this sub-
lime, mysterious goddess figure, Whitman uses both connotative me-
ters. Two pentameters, appropriately enough, evoke the presence of
the literary giants "gathering around" in the first two lines. The dac-
tyls in the line about their "masterful eyes" may have something to
do with their effect on the Mother of All, whose gracious response
is described in two long dactylic lines before her exit, lines akin to
those that evoke the archetypal feminine rhythm of the sea in "Out
of the Cradle Endlessly Rocking." The picture of this dactylic crea-
ture pausing, "blent with their music," in appreciation of the iambic
pentameter's "great shadowy groups gathering round," is a picture
of metrical harmony.

At the conclusion of "Proud Music of the Storm" the two differ-
ent meters not only harmonize, but fuse into a powerful ideal for a
new poetry. The poet has been dreaming of hearing a variety of
musical sounds. Some are typically dactylic, such as "the primitive
chants of the Nile boatmen, / The sacred imperial hymns of China."
Some are typically iambic, such as "I hear religious dances old and
new." The coexistence of such different kinds of music, including
metrical music, in one dream prepares the way for the final passage
of the poem. Here the poet explains to his soul that the "music of
my dream" has not been made of ordinary, familiar sounds—the
"vocalism of sun-bright Italy," a "German organ majestic," the
"sound of marching soldiers," but of something new:

a new rhythmus fitted for thee,
Poems bridging the way from Life to Death, vaguely wafted in night
    air, uncaught, unwritten,
Which let us go forth in the bold day and write.

On the metrical level, this "new rhythmus" is not made out of whole cloth, but consists of the harmonious cooperation between iambic pentameter and dactylic rhythms explored elsewhere in Whitman. The penultimate line moves from an initial embedded metapentameter, "Poems bridging the way from Life to Death," to a classic Whitmanian dactylic passage that evokes vagueness, night, and the unspeakable. In this poem, however, the ineffable dactylic power is openly seized in the final, iambic pentameter line. The final line promises to speak the unspeakable, to write the unwriteable, to bridge life and death—to bring the suggestive power of the dactylic rhythm into cooperation with the explicit, traditionally grounded confidence of the pentameter.

Of all the varied and conflicting proposed theories about Whitman's prosody, few have placed him in any meaningful relation to the poetic tradition with which he himself was most intimately connected: that of America and Britain through the mid–nineteenth century.[9] Like Dickinson, Whitman tends to be thought an oddity who developed virtually independently of the poems that were being written around him. Assumptions about meter may play a larger part in these kinds of categorizations than is at first obvious. Each poet's metrical practice is considered anomalous; the poet is therefore distanced from other poets on the basis of the very quality that, traditionally and arguably, most distinguishes poetry from prose.

As a result, the two poets currently ranked as the greatest in nineteenth-century America are oddities—a view that has not had the best effect on their individual reputations, nor perhaps on that of American poetry generally. More energy, on the whole, has been spent examining both of these poets' legendary personalities than giving serious and rigorous criticism to the poetry itself. When poetry is considered so special that it precludes demanding criticism, the line between awe and condescension can become surprisingly thin.[10] And when Whitman's work is treated as a phenomenon completely separate from Longfellow's, or Dickinson's poems as utterly unrelated to those of her more sentimental contemporary Helen Hunt Jackson, the former poets furnish a facile justification for blindness to the merits of the latter, and American poetry as a whole is diminished.

The metrical code shows that metrically variable verse in America has not been as dissevered from more traditional verse as it may appear. The crucial point is not only that, as Lois Ware, Basil de Selincourt, and others have pointed out, Whitman wrote conventionally metrical lines. The point is that the conventional metrical lines in *Leaves of Grass* are charged with specific, culturally created meanings. Whatever the level of consciousness involved on the part of the poet, this fact makes it harder to claim, with de Selincourt, that "clearly Whitman's refusal of metre was the refusal [i.e., result] of innocence, not of experience" (72). If metrical-code analysis modifies somewhat the conception of Whitman as a rude, autochthonous anomaly, it may lend him a more realistic and dignified place within the larger history of poetry in English.

Chapter 4

Stephen Crane and the Rhythms of the 1890s

Stephen Crane's little book, *The Black Riders and Other Lines,* which appeared in 1895, was the first significant volume of free verse to be published in America after *Leaves of Grass.* Its technique is radically different from Whitman's. Rhythmic momentum is rare within lines or poems; the poems themselves are extremely short, the cadences singularly flat, and the tone detached. Only eight lines in the entire book sustain their meter long enough to constitute an iambic pentameter, and virtually no complete lines appear in less common rhythms. The poems seem on the surface to have no particular metrical characteristics at all.

But if the rhythms of *The Black Riders* are examined on the level of the metrical foot rather than on that of the line, the poems contain a surprising amount of metrical activity. Iambic and triple meters interact in similar patterns throughout the poems. Furthermore, the metrical-code associations of individual iambs and dactyls clearly correspond to iambic-pentameter and dactylic associations in Dickinson and Whitman. Crane consistently associates iambic feet with conventional, culturally accepted values, although he responds to these values more negatively than do the two earlier poets. Most of Whitman and Dickinson's association of the iambic pentameter with authority and strength has dropped away in Crane, leaving only a bitter disillusionment that presages the widespread move to free verse in the early twentieth century.

Crane's attitudes towards the dactylic rhythm also relate closely to Whitman's. Reflecting the more general prosodic attitude of his time, Crane's ambivalence towards the dactyl is stronger. On the

other hand, the dactyl in Crane opposes the iamb more vehemently
than it does in Whitman, and the possibility of cooperation between
them is far more distant than in the earlier poet.

Poem 19, for example, shows a pronounced fear of triple feet,
which involve violent force, while it associates the pentameter with
a contemptible conformity:

> Ă gód| ĭn wráth
> Wăs beát|ĭng ă mán;
> Hĕ cúffed| hĭm loúd|lў
> Wĭth thún|dĕroŭs blóws
> Thăt ráng| ănd rŏlled óv|ĕr thĕ eárth.
> Ăll| peóple căme| rúnnĭng.
> Thĕ| mán scréamed ănd| strúgglĕd
> Ănd bĭt mád|lў ăt thĕ feét| ŏf thĕ gód.
> Thĕ peó|plĕ crièd:| "Ăh, whát| ă wíck|ĕd mán!"
> And—
> "Àh,| whát ă rĕ|doúbtăblĕ| gód!"

The triple measure builds from the poem's first few lines—"beating
a man," "thunderous blows," "rang and rolled over," through the
metrical climax in two rhythmically equivalent lines, the sixth and
seventh, to the admiring dactyls in the last line. As the man bites
"madly at the feet of the god," the triple rhythm is exaggerated by
the addition of another unstressed syllable; finally, though, the voice
of social convention reproaches it in the antepenultimate iambic pen-
tameter.

How much Crane's poetry owes to Whitman's influence on any
level is arguable.[1] Daniel Hoffman remarks,

> Crane . . . would seem to have taken over so little of Whitman's
> thought and diction as to raise the possibilities either that he had
> read very little of Whitman's verse, or that what similarities exist
> between that verse and his own may result not from direct
> influences but from analogous responses. (211)

No theories of direct influence, however, are needed in order to ex-
plain the kinship between metrical connotations in Crane and
Whitman: Whitman's impact might easily have reached Crane indi-
rectly. As a poet committed to metrically variable verse at a time
when such verse was rare, Crane is also likely to have been deeply

and originally sensitive, like Whitman, to metrical associations and traditions. The subtlety of Crane's metrical interaction as opposed to Whitman's stems from the radically different prosodic forces at work in his era. While Whitman discovered his prosody during a time of new possibilities in meter, Crane produced his poems during a period of more debilitating metrical crisis.

Whitman's prosodic influence is generally believed to have "passed to France," to the French symbolists, around the time of his death (Allen, *American Prosody* 242). From there it would return to revolutionize American poetic technique in turn, through the influence of the French poets on American modernism. Such a model explains the apparent lack of significant Whitmanian echoes in the poetry of fin-de-siècle America. It is easy to view the period, presided over by metrically conservative poets such as Bayard Taylor and William Vaughn Moody, simply as an era of "conservative reasser-tion" (Edwin Fussell 34).

But "the twilight years," as the nineties are often called, were not as metrically homogenous as they may appear.[2] In 1892 the young Edwin Arlington Robinson lamented Whitman's passing, in iambs so relentless that they seem deliberately to express a sense of metrical deprivation:

> The master-songs are ended, and the man
> that sang them is a name. . . .
> We do not hear him very much today:
> His piercing and eternal cadence rings
> Too pure for us—too powerfully pure,
> Too lovingly triumphant, and too large;
> But there are some that hear him.

Even in his gloomy elegy, Robinson must admit that Whitman is not completely forgotten. The "some that hear him" in Robinson's poem included Whitman's admirers John Burroughs, Richard Bucke, and William O'Connor, all of whom continued to write "Whitmanics," as George Saintsbury named them (*History* 492). Whitman had, in the words of Carlin Kindilien, "more of a vogue [in America in the 1890s] than has been suspected"; a whole school of minor poets con-tinued to be inspired by both his ideas and his forms (197). Hamlin Garland's 1893 *Prairie Songs,* in varied rhymed and unrhymed forms, featured a tribute to Whitman. Even the Harvard poet George Cabot

Lodge experimented with Whitmanesque free verse, right along with Swinburnian meters and French forms, in his 1898 volume *The Song of the Wave* (Stauffer 204) and dedicated his second volume, *Poems,* to Whitman the following year (Folsom xxviii).

Still, the general reception of Whitman's verse as poetry by the 1890s—irregular poetry or prose poetry perhaps, but still poetry—did not make Crane's emergence as a poet much easier. When *The Black Riders and Other Lines* appeared in 1895, most reviewers, including those who liked the book, did not deign to call it poetry at all. The *Daily Tribune*'s critic puts it simply: "sudden or not, the visitation to which we owe Mr. Crane's 'lines' does not seem to have come from Parnassus" (Review of *The Black Riders* 65). The reviewer for *Munsey's Magazine,* a publication that was later to think highly of Crane's novels, scorns the *The Black Riders:*

> Because a man has genius, there is no reason for his being encouraged in making alleged poetry that is without rhyme or meter. If he has not learned the mechanical secrets of his trade, his work cannot be sufficiently finished to be worthy of acceptance. (66)

The assumption underlying such criticisms of *The Black Riders qua* poetry was the common understanding that, in the words of another anonymous reviewer, "rhythm is as essential to poetry as grammar is to prose" (Review of *The Black Riders, New York Daily Tribune* 66). Of the more sophisticated reviewers who lauded the book, only Harry Peck in *The Bookman* ignores the issue of its genre definition altogether, calling Crane clearly a poet—an "original, and powerful writer of eccentric verse" (65). William Dean Howells, thirty years after defining Whitman's verse as rhythmic prose, had stretched his criteria for poetry somewhat—but not enough to accommodate Crane without qualification. In his review of *The Black Riders,* Howells skirts the genre question first by appealing to relativism and finally by claiming that form is really irrelevant to the issue at hand:

> I myself would not have chosen Mr. Crane's form because it is so near formlessness, and because I would rather live in a house of the accepted structure than in a hut of logs and boughs. But I do not pronounce my preference in this as a law. . . . after all,

how a man gives you his thought is not so important as what thought he gives you. (70–71)

While he retains an implicit hierarchy by calling Crane's writing a "hut" as opposed to the house of formal poetry, Howells concludes his review by printing a Crane poem as prose, in order to show that it "owes nothing of its poetry to the typographic mask of metre" (72). Thomas Wentworth Higginson, who knew too much about poetry to dismiss meter as a typographic mask, handles the issue with more grace and perhaps more astuteness by describing the book in terms of its "covert rhythm" (68).

According to the most established wisdom of the time— Whitman notwithstanding—poetry was still poetry by virtue of its meter. In 1893 Yale professor Albert S. Cook reissued Leigh Hunt's 1844 essay, "An Answer to the Question 'What is Poetry?' including Remarks on Versification," for use by the college students of the nineties. Meter, defined in the phrase "variety in uniformity," is essential to Hunt's view of poetry

> not merely as poetic feeling, which is more or less shared by all the world, but as the operation of that feeling . . . the utterance of a passion for truth, beauty, and power, embodying and illustrating its conceptions by imagination and fancy, . . . modulating its language on the principle of variety in uniformity. (1)

If anything, the definitions of poetry at the end of the century tended to concentrate on the last part of Hunt's definition as the most crucial. Edmund Clarence Stedman, in the introduction to his influential 1900 anthology of American poetry, pronounces that poetry is "rhythmical expression" (xxix). Francis Gummere's *The Beginnings of Poetry* sees "in rhythm, or regularity of recurrence due to the consenting cadence of a throng, the main representative of communal forces" that give poetry its power (465).

But at the same time, a tendency was underway to define poetry in terms of the first part of Hunt's definition at the expense of the latter part—as a matter, not of form, but of something theoretically more essential. Emerson had explicitly distinguished the "true poet" from mere "men of poetical talents, or of industry and skill in metre." Accentuating the movement towards common speech started by the first English Romantics, he asserted that "it is not metres, but a metre-making argument, that makes a poem,—a thought so passion-ate and alive, that . . . it has an architecture of its own" (266). In 1886 George Raymond argues, in the same tradition, that "poetry is an artistic development of language; its versification, of the pauses of natural breathing," and from this concludes that "this inference neces-sarily carries with it another . . . that no effects produced by sound are legitimate in poetry, which fail in any degree to represent thought" (150). The assertion that a poem's form should (and could) be deter-mined by its content rather than by its genre forms the basis not only for Howells's relegating of meter to the status of a mask but, more importantly, for his decision that the words of Crane's poems will be proved stronger and better if they can be read effectively as prose. Howells apparently believes that prose form is inherently more "or-ganic" (to use the twentieth-century term) than poetic meter, and he was followed by decades of twentieth-century poets who took good prose style as a model for poetry and, subscribing to the doctrine of "organic form," wrote without explicitly "modulating their language on the principle of variety in uniformity."

While the Romantics were establishing the primacy of content over form, another nineteenth-century development pushed poetry away from regular meter from a completely different direction.[3] For the first time since the Renaissance, poets became interested in reviv-ing classical quantitative measures, particularly the dactylic hexame-ter. From Southey to Longfellow, Tennyson, Arnold, and Bridges, they struggled to make English stress-prosody fit the classical sylla-ble-length patterns in ways that might capture the feeling of classical poetry, or at least might provide English poetry with new kinds of viable meters. It was generally agreed that while the English language provided hardly any spondees—vital to the classical hexameter—tro-chees would be an acceptable substitute.[4] Other problems, not so easily resolved, centered on the general question of whether the dac-tylic foot—or the English stress equivalent of the quantitative dactylic foot—was appropriate at all in English poetry.

In spite of the practice of such poets as Longfellow, Whitman, and Crane—and even in spite of Matthew Arnold's conviction, ex-pressed in the 1860 lectures *On Translating Homer,* that "there is no reason in the English language why it should not adapt itself to hex-ameters" (103)—a profound discomfort about the very existence of the dactylic foot is evident in many late–nineteenth-century writings about prosody. Richard Garnett, arguing in 1901 that the optimum form for translating Homer into English is the heroic couplet, at first rejects conventional English dactylic hexameters because they tend to move too fast and the stresses are hard to control. Having found instead a "rhymed and curtailed" hexameter that he claims to like very much, he criticizes this form in turn because of "an undeniable tinge of eccentricity," suggesting that the dactylic meter gives the translation in question an archaic tone and might even "tend to generate" the odd language to which the translator is prone (11–16). Even after professing an exceptional admiration for this dactylic translation, Garnett dismisses its meter easily, with very little discussion; his glibness suggests that the critical climate was sympathetic to such a dismissal of the dactyl. In the same year, William Hand Browne records that several prosodists have called Milton's dactylic line "Burnt after them to the bottomless pit" a "harsh" line, without even noticing that the line has three dactyls and is hence "alien" to the blank verse context (198).[5] The word *harsh* suggests a purely aesthetic antipathy to the dactylic meter. Even Gummere, after listing some successful modern dactylic hexameter poems in his *Handbook of Poetics,* puts his acknowledgment of their value in terms of a fight; he can only say that "at least [they] should make us recognize this measure as a belligerent" (230).

In spite of his tendency to metrical experiments, Swinburne also had hard words for the dactyl. Saintsbury quotes the poet, in a note to "Studies in Song," observing that "all variations and combinations of anapestic, iambic, or trochaic meter are as natural and pliable [to English] as all dactylic and spondaic forms of verse are unnatural and abhorrent" (qtd. in *History* 352). Saintsbury himself finds nothing wrong with the English hexameter in terms of objective form—he judges it "in form a fairly adequate equivalent of the Latin hexameter"—but dismisses the meter vehemently nonetheless:

Only, this equivalent [to the classical hexameter] is in totally wrong *material*—material which rings false, at every beat and echo, when the whole line, and several lines, are taken together, it seems to me . . . to be the equivalent of nothing at all except the most floundering and unrhythmical doggerel. (*History* 399)

Saintsbury solves the apparent contradiction between his and
Swinburne's views of the dactyl and the latter's apparent use of it by
the rather elaborate recourse of scanning lines that appear to be dac-
tylic hexameters instead as "a five-anapest line with anacrusis [an
extra initial syllable] and hypercatalexis [extra final syllables]" (*History*
414). Claiming that "the dactylic rhythm [is] difficult, if not impos-
sible, to keep up in our language," Saintsbury elsewhere disposes of
"the various attempts at 'hexameters' in English" in a few pages; he
finds that Longfellow's dactyls at their best give an anapestic effect,
and calls the hexameter of *Evangeline* "an essentially rickety measure"
(*Historical Manual* 120–23). Elsewhere, in a revealingly judgmental
phrase, Saintsbury calls Swinburne's sapphics "more touchy" than
his hexameters because the dactylic feet in the sapphics cannot be
explained away in scansion (423).

Most of these attacks against the dactyl evince a surprising level
of emotional motivation. If nothing else, the energy expended in the
many discussions of English dactyls attests to the strong attraction
exerted by the "3-rhythm" or triple foot, a measure for which Sidney
Lanier claims in *The Science of English Verse* (1880) that the English
ear has always had "an overpowering passion" (110). Whitman's
prosody probably had no small influence on this statement; Donald
Stauffer considers Lanier's own dactylic poetry to have been strongly
influenced by a "belated reading of Whitman" several years before
Lanier published this opinion (128).

Perhaps demonstrating such a passion, as well as a violent re-
sponse to the prosodic demands of the dactyl, Carl Benson uses a
peculiar and ambivalent metaphor to describe the faulty quality of
"one of Schiller's *dactylic apologies*" according to the rules of classical
scansion:

> I say again, that a syllable ending in three such consonants cannot
> be made a weak syllable. You may cram it into the place of one,
> as Cinderella's sister crammed her foot into the slipper, but the
> line will suffer from it as much as she did. (483)

In the Grimm Brothers' version of the story, Cinderella's sister en-
gaged in self-mutilation, cutting off her toes in order to make her
foot fit into the gorgeous slipper. She finally bled so much that the
prince discovered her deception. The violence of Benson's metaphor

reveals an extreme degree of frustration at the difficulty of making modern language stress behave according to a classical pattern. Later, in a discussion of the English equivalent to Latin dactylic pentameter, Benson attacks the dactylic hexameter again:

> A succession of [these lines] usually becomes tedious, prosaic, and eminently *sticky*. Show one of the ordinary specimens . . . to any gentleman of your acquaintance who is not fresh in his classics, and ten to one he will read it as prose, and not be able to detect any metre in it. (484)

Benson's equation of the dactylic measure with prose—presumably a cutting insult—may help to explain the prevalent impatience with dactyls. By making demands counter to the habitual demands of iambic rhythm, dactyls seemed to force the English language, making it feel less naturally rhythmical, less "poetic."[6] In "Hexameters and Rhythmic Prose," published in 1890, George Palmer clearly asserts a connection between dactylic measures and prose. After remarking that "a tendency to alternate accent [i.e., an iambic tendency] is deep in the temper of the [English] language," he concludes that because of its length and many permissible variations,

> I cannot think there is a question that the hexameter strikes us all as a species of prose which has advanced a good way into the country of verse, or as verse temporarily sojourning in the regions of prose. (526–27)

Palmer ends his discussion of the dactylic hexameter by abandoning the meter altogether and offering his translation of the *Odyssey* in iambically measured prose.

Recently, the theory of triple rhythm as a descendent of strong-stress verse has offered one very plausible explanation for the reaction against dactyls in English. According to ideas advanced by Martin Halpern and by Edward Weissmuller, strong-stress meter works on completely different principles from accentual-syllabic meter. Unlike the stresses in accentual-syllabic meter, the stresses in strong-stress meter are isoaccentual and isochronous—all are equally strong and take equally long to pronounce. Because of this fundamental opposition between the two meters, Weissmuller thinks they "had been struggling all along to keep their separateness" (282). According to Weissmuller, when they could no longer do so, and the two different prosodic principles merged in the same poems, the metrical result was free verse (287).

In this schema, it is no wonder that poets and prosodists struck out at the English dactylic measure and called it eccentric, alien, doggerel, prose.[7] And perhaps, it is no wonder that simultaneously they were attracted to it. The dactylic measure posed a real and irresistible threat to the basis of all post-Renaissance English poetry. On the other hand, it offered a way out of a poetic era that seemed mediocre even to itself. As Stedman put it in 1900, "we have minor voices and their tentative modes and tones" ("Introduction" xxviii).

Whitman's reputation during this time was paradoxical; he was admired to a much greater extent than he was imitated. Poets such as Robert Buchanan and Joaquin Miller, for example, wrote Whitman many warm tributes in rigidly conventional metrical verse whose form seems to belie his influence (Folsom xxiv, xxvii).[8] The singular nature of Whitman's prosody offers one likely explanation for the success of his reputation in spite of his radical free-verse practice. Whitman's triple rhythms, unlike the dactylic hexameters that caused so much controversy among nineteenth-century critics—even for the immensely popular Longfellow—were syllabically irregular.[9] His dactyls insinuated themselves into American poetry without catching themselves on the rules of quasi-classical scansion or the real or imagined difficulties of fitting English to dactylic patterns. Since they were not regularly metrical, they didn't explicitly threaten the iambic accentual-syllabic base of the poetry around them. Whitman's singular prosody, which could pass for prose, allowed readers to indulge in a taste for dactyls without seeming to compromise prosodic conventions. Even in this poetically conservative era, when Whitman's influence was less than before or since, his prosody did not prevent him from appealing to readers and—once he had gained it—from keeping the title of "poet."

Unlike Crane's, Whitman's poetry is conspicuously rhythmic. In fact, his "rhythmic prose" or "prosaic poetry" won arguments for proponents of each genre. In a notorious controversy in the *The Gentleman's Magazine,* Arthur Clive used Whitman as his main evidence for the superiority of prose over poetry, arguing that Whitman was "a great poet [who has] deliberately chosen to express himself in plain prose without invoking the aid either of rhyme or rhythm in any of its forms" (184). According to Clive, Whitman proves that prose is both more "natural" and more "mature" than poetry and should completely replace it (195–96). In a reply intended to defend meter as crucial to poetry, the prosodist T. S. Omond made Whitman his primary evidence on the other side of the argument by pointing out that Whitman himself did not avoid slipping into meter: "whenever the thoughts are earnest and glowing and 'poetical,' the language instantly assumes a metrical cadence" (349).

In the face of Whitman's increasingly powerful reputation, Crane's choice to abandon even the irregular Whitmanian species of rhythm testifies to a growing impasse between dactylic tendencies and the established metrical system. Larzer Ziff speaks of poets in the 1890s as caught in "a stalemate of two traditions—that of Whitman and that of Victorian English verse—whose conflicts rendered their inheritors powerless to find a way out of the twilight time" (314). This wider poetic conflict emerges in Crane's use of various free-verse rhythms that echo metrical feet; in Crane, the forces of Whitmanian and traditional English verse manifest themselves metrically as triple feet and iambs.[10] Crane, because of his sensitivity to the conflicting pulls of two metrical systems that were essentially in the process of neutralizing each other, was a key figure in the development of twentieth-century free verse.

Whitman also embodied the tension between iambs and triple rhythms—particularly dactyls—but he did so at a point when the metrical contrast meant exciting poetic possibilities rather than a stalemate of traditions. For Crane, the conflicting metrical forces forestalled rhythmic expression instead of enhancing it. The contrast parallels a larger difference between the attitudes towards poetry held by these two prosodic rebels. Whitman considered himself a poet and located himself within a tradition of poets. Crane, on the other hand, wrote to Nellie Crouse after receiving an invitation to a dinner to honor his poetic genius: "I was very properly enraged at the word 'poet' which continually reminds me of long-hair and seems to me to be a most detestable form of insult" (*Letters* 85). Crane referred to the writings in *The Black Riders and Other Lines* as "lines" or "pills," not as "poems." Whitman's explicit relation to biblical prosodic structures gives him an unorthodox but still "poetic" genealogy, while Cady points out that—in spite of the story that Crane was struck by Dickinson's poems when they were shown him by William Dean Howells—it is impossible, when analyzing Crane's poems, "to find true sources for them as poems" (116). The fact that Crane's poems reflect the metrical conflicts of his time in spite of his self-imposed distance from poetry argues for the pervasive influence of those conflicts in the 1890s.

Crane's and Whitman's metrical attitudes relate to larger differences in philosophy as well as to their different prosodic environments and poetic self-definitions. Unlike Whitman, Crane did not have the kind of belief in free will that might have led him to assert a strong poetic cadence in despite of all tradition. Daniel Hoffman contrasts the two poets thus:

> In Crane we see the isolato in a deterministic world; man is made infinitesimal by the hugeness of natural forces against which he struggles, not to impose his will, but to live in accordance with a code that allows him dignity despite his insignificance. . . . Whitman, on the other hand, shows us the isolato in a world where necessity is absent and the will is free—free to reassert the power of the self to reenter the world from which it would seem to have been barred by the very forces which isolated it. (216–17)

This passage can stand as a description of the two poets' metrical strategies. Whitman, flying in the face of all consistency, asserts the urgent power of dactylic rhythm even as he maintains the authority of iambic pentameter and denies all metrical patterns with prose rhythms that led some of his contemporaries not to hear his rhythms at all. But Crane asserts no particular rhythm, instead reflecting and exploring the conflict between dactyls and iambs that he has inherited. Crane could have been speaking of his meter when he said that "every artist must be in some things powerless as a dead snake" (qtd. in Berryman 6). He embodies metrical tension as only a fatalist could.

Much of *The Black Riders* can be read as a dialogue between iambs and triple feet. In certain of the poems, interaction between iambs and dactyls is mediated by the anapestic rhythm which, as a rising rhythm like the iamb but a triple rhythm like the dactyl, has a bridging function. Crane's verse is difficult to scan consistently; the delineation of metrical qualities is at best problematic in free verse as irregular as his, since meter arguably must, by definition, involve regularly repeated patterns. But the rhythms of Crane's free verse reward the effort to associate them with metrical feet; the connotations of his iambic, dactylic, and anapestic rhythms form consistent patterns related to the practice of previous, more regularly metrical poets.

My scansions of Crane's triple feet attempt to capture a highly characteristic rhythm that recurs briefly but quite often throughout the poems in *The Black Riders*. I arrive at the scansions of dactylic as opposed to anapestic feet in two ways: sometimes by the more usual method, scanning from the beginning of the line, but sometimes by scanning from the end of the line. The latter technique, bracketing off the line's initial unstressed syllable instead of its final unstressed syllable, makes clear what are, to my ear, some of Crane's most distinctive and moving rhythms: the strong falling cadences in a line like "tradition, thou art for suckling children."[11] Such "scansions," of course, are based on the actual stress patterns of Crane's word choices and do not involve any kind of counterpointing. Their foot boundaries generally correspond to word and phrase boundaries, as they do in the line quoted above.[12]

Crane's iambic feet are consistent in their associations with the few actual iambic pentameter lines in *The Black Riders*. Read according to the metrical-code theory, these pentameters reveal an intense disillusionment with the predominant metric of the Victorian tradition, and by extension with traditional poetic endeavors. Three of the eight iambic pentameters in the book emphasize bleakness and futility: "I saw a man pursuing the horizon" (poem 24); "I saw a creature naked, bestial" (poem 3); "And ultimately he died, thus, alone" (poem 17). Three others express consciousness of the danger of taking on powerful forces: "And it is not fine for gods to menace fools" (poem 13); "A-start at threatening faces of the past" (poem 63); "There was a man who lived a life of fire" (poem 62).

The tone of the two other pentameters is more consistent with the usual tone of iambic feet in Crane's poetry; they express a weak and conventional attitude. In the split pentameter in poem 19, discussed above, the iambic pentameter conformity that caused Whitman some ambivalence about the meter has become so compliant that it is arguably evil:

A god in wrath
Was beating a man;
He cuffed him loudly
With thunderous blows
That rang and rolled over the earth.
All people came running.
The man screamed and struggled,
And bit madly at the feet of the god.
The people cried:
"Ah, what a wicked man!"
And—
"Ah, what a redoubtable god!"

The absence of any apparent justification for the god's treatment of the man in this scene makes the people's reverence for the god horrifying and their willingness to condemn the man even more so. The split pentameter, "The people cried, / 'Ah, what a wicked man!,'" describes an automatic response of complicity with evil that adds chilling associations of betrayal and collusion with power to Crane's iambic pentameters. The last pentameter concludes poem 31, a narrative about workmen who put a huge ball of masonry on a mountaintop, turn to admire it, and are then suddenly crushed as it falls on them: "It crushed them all to blood. / But some had opportunity to squeal." The use of pentameter in the bizarre final line might suggest, again, that the meter's intimacy with oppressive forces—in this case, an association more pathetic than evil—allows the squealers their opportunity.

Poem 26 can be read in terms of the habitual associations of all three metrical feet: the iambs as poetic tradition, the dactyls compelling and torturing the poet with their sublime inapproachability, and the anapests as a bridge. The poem's opening line of alternating anapests and iambs presents a challenge for the speaker:

Thĕre wăs sét| bĕfóre| mĕ ă míght|lў híll,
Ănd lóng dáys| Ĭ clímbed
Thróugh ré|giŏns ŏf snów.
Whĕn Ĭ hád| bĕfóre| mĕ thĕ súm|mĭt-viéw,
Ĭt| seémed thăt mў| lábŏr
Hăd| beén tŏ seé| gárdĕns
Lýĭng ăt ĭm|póssĭblĕ| dístăncĕs.

This initial line sets the challenge of traditional, rising English rhythms before the poet; the iambs seem to give the hill its verticality because they contain the crucial information that challenges the poet, the phrase "before [me]" and the word "hill" itself. The next few lines are primarily spondaic (as David Halliburton has pointed out, spondaic measures are common in Crane [477])[13] but preserve a rising rhythm with the iambic undercurrent in line 2 and the anapest in line 3; they are transitional lines. Line 4 duplicates exactly the rhythm of line 1, metrically making the point that no progress has really been made, but the visions of the distant gardens in the last three lines are presented in dactylic rhythms.

Such evocations of beautiful but inaccessible dactyls are repeated again and again in *The Black Riders*. In poem 28, two travelers describe truth. Each description is introduced by the dactylic opening, "'Truth,' said a| tráveller," establishing the relation between dactyls and truth that will persist throughout the poem. The first traveler claims to have been to Truth's highest tower, "From whence| the world| looks black"—a perception expressed in unequivocal iambs. The second traveler, whom the speaker says he believes, says of truth:

Lòng have| I pursued| it,
But nev|er have| I touched
The| hém of its| gármĕnt.

Lóng have| I pur|sued it,
But| never| have I| touched

The first and second lines here are metrically ambiguous; each can be read as having a rising or a falling undercurrent. The description of the hem of truth's garment, however, like the description of the gardens at impossible distances, follows the pattern of the majority of Crane's dactylic lines: an unstressed syllable followed by a dactyl and a trochee. When the poem's narrator declares that he believes the second traveler rather than the first, he repeats the second traveler's description of truth, but not exactly. He omits the antepenultimate line of the traveler's description:

For truth was to me
A breath, a wind,
A| shádŏw, a| phántŏm,
And never had I touched
The| hém of its| gármĕnt.

Metrically, the result of this omission is that a dactylic line on the exact pattern of the last line—"A shadow, a phantom"—replaces the metrically ambiguous line "Long have I pursued it." This substitution gives a much stronger dactylic rhythm to the closing description of truth. Since the speaker has actually had a chance to accept a more definite (and iambic) view of truth at this point but has rejected it, truth is even more inaccessible on the poem's thematic level than it was formerly. The stronger dactylic rhythm corresponds to this greater inaccessibility.

In poem 65, the dactyls describe little birds that the speaker holds in a (trochaic) basket:

> And Ĭ| hĕld thĕm| ĭn ă| báskĕt.
> Whĕn Ĭ óp|ĕnĕd thĕ wíck|ĕt,
> Heávĕns! thĕy| áll flĕw ă|wáy.
> I cried, "Come back, little thoughts!"
> But they only laughed.
> They flew on
> Until they were as sand
> Thrówn bĕtwĕen| mĕ ănd thĕ| ský.

Like the image of the basket holding birds, the trochee holds the falling rhythm of the dactyl within the tight double beat of the iamb. Like the speaker opening the basket, the anapest opens from the iamb into the triple rhythm of the dactyl. When the birds fly away, they do so in two rhythmically identical lines, each consisting of two dactyls and a final additional stress. In the first of these dactylic lines the birds become inaccessible, and in the second they are confusing, obscure, thrown between the speaker and the sky.

Dactyls, which Whitman used to urge his soul to fly like a bird in "A Song of Joys," are also associated with birds in poem 2, "Thrée líttlĕ| bírds ĭn ă| rów." The three little dactylic birds contrast with an iambic human ("ă mán| pàssed neár| thăt pláce"); they are described as "vérў| cúriŏus," explicitly evoking the quality of strangeness in many of Crane's dactyls. In poem 34, for instance, "mánў strănge| pédlărs" come to the speaker, "hóldĭng| fórth líttlĕ| ímăgĕs,| sáyĭng;| / Thís ĭs mў| páttĕrn ŏf| Gód." The speaker answers them:

> Bŭt Ĭ| sàid "Héncĕ!
> Lĕávĕ mé| wĭth mĭne ówn.

Ănd táke| yŏu yóurs| ăwáy;
Ĭ căn't búy| ŏf yŏur pát|tĕrns ŏf Gód,
Thĕ lít|tlĕ góds| yŏu mắy right|lў prĕfér.

The speaker's rejection of the strange gods is in rising rhythms: the conventional iambs that usually embody received wisdom and steadfast human normalcy in Crane, and anapests, introducing a note of relativism and a bridge to the dactyl.

In poem 39, dactyls are associated with a direct spirituality that is so quiet it is almost inaccessible, even though it is internal. This spirituality contrasts with a more extravagant, externalized, primarily iambic spirituality:

Thĕ lív|ĭd líght|nĭngs fláshed| ĭn thĕ clóuds;
Thĕ léad|ĕn thún|dĕrs cráshed.
Ă wór|shĭppĕr raísed| hĭs árm.
"Heárkĕn!| Heárkĕn!| Thĕ vóice| ŏf Gód!"

"Nòt só,"| saĭd ă mán.
"Thĕ vóice| ŏf Gód| whíspĕrs ĭn| thĕ heárt
Sŏ sóftly
Thăt thĕ sóul| páusĕs,
Mákĭng nŏ| nóise,
Ănd| stríves fŏr thĕse| mélŏdĭĕs,
Dístănt,| síghĭng,| lĭke faín|tĕst bréath,
Ănd áll| thĕ bé|ĭng ĭs stíll| tŏ heár.

The dactyls in this poem begin with the evocation of the quiet internality of God: "whispers in." Further dactyls describe the soul pausing, then striving for "these melodies"—powerful, though difficult to hear among the predominantly rising rhythms.

In poem 46, an inner state in triple meter again opposes an outer iambic state, although in this case the triple feet express an inner psychological truth rather than the spiritual truth of the dactyls above: "Mánў rĕd| dévĭls| rán frŏm mў| heárt / Ănd óut| ŭpón| thĕ páge." The contrast between the dactylic self-knowledge and the external iambic act of writing is reiterated at the end of the poem, although now that the inner condition has been more externalized, the triple foot is anapestic rather than dactylic: "Tŏ wríte| ĭn thís| rèd múck / Ŏf thíngs| frŏm mў heárt." In poem 62, the contrast between appearance and inner truth takes a different form; a man's life glows, to all outward (iambic) appearances "ă dĭre| rĕd stáin,| ĭndél|ĭblĕ"; but when he is dead, "hĕ sáw| thăt hĕ hád| nŏt lived." The sole anapest in the last line, read in the context of Crane's other triple feet, asserts even more strongly the inner truth of the dead man's insight.

In spite of the several poems where Crane opposes the iambic norm with a precious inner truth in triple feet, his attitude towards triple feet is ambivalent more often than not. Most of the poems involving triple feet concern the difficulty or impossibility of listening to inner truth; frequently the speaker resists the triple force as much as he is drawn to it. In poem 7, for instance, a single dactyl expresses the speaker's fear that the actual truth will be bitter: "Ănd— téll| mĕ—ĭs| ĭt fáir / Ŏr ĭs| thĕ trúth| bíttĕr ăs| eátĕn| fíre?" In poem 6, the first four lines describe God's creation of "the ship of the world" in dactylic rhythm, strengthening the connection of dactyls with spirituality; but after the ship has slipped away from God, the dactyls take on another character as they describe the ship

> Góĭng rĭ|dícŭlŏus| vóyăgĕs,
> Mákĭng quàint| prógrĕss,
> Túrnĭng ăs wĭth| sérĭŏus| púrpŏse
> Bĕfóre| stúpĭd| wínds.

The dactyls now appear ridiculous, divorced from God and left to their own devices; they keep the appearance of sacred seriousness, but are actually at the mercy of the "stupid" prevailing iambic and trochaic winds.

Fear of being at the mercy of the sublime force of the dactyl, as opposed to the anapest, is eloquent in poem 66:

> Ĭf Ĭ| shŏuld cást| ŏff thĭs tát|tĕred cóat
> Ănd gŏ frée| ĭntó| thĕ míght|lў skу́;
> Ĭf Ĭ| shŏuld fínd| nŏthĭng thére
> Bŭt ă| vást blúe,
> Échŏlĕss,| ígnŏrănt,—
> Whăt thén?

The poem is written completely in anapests and iambs except for the fourth and fifth lines, where a "vast blue" spondee introduces the frighteningly uncontrolled "echoless, ignorant" dactylic spectacle. The last line is, appropriately, a single iamb, representing a voice of conventional human apprehension expressed in a common speech idiom.

The unconventionality of the intense religious and philosophical power in Crane's triple feet may explain the marked ambivalence or even hostility towards them in his poems, paralleling that in the prosodic writings of the period. In poem 27, the "quaint" quality of the ship "mákǐng quàint| prógrěss" in poem 6 recurs in association with triple feet. Both a "yóuth iň ǎp|párěl thǎt| glǐttěred" and an assassin, "ǎt|tíred aľl iň| gárb ǒf thě| óld dàys" whose "dággěr pǒised| quǐvěriňg," are described in triple feet, which here have the same kind of horrifying potential that Whitman evokes with dactyls in the "blood-dripping wounds" of "Lo, Victress on the Peaks." When the youth accepts his own murder with the remarkable statement, "Í ǎm eň|chántěd, bě|líeve mè" to die "Ín thǐs mě|dievǎl| fáshiǒn, / Accórd-iňg tǒ| thě bést| légěnds," the complicity between the youth and his assassin remains until the youth dies ("Thěn tóok| hě thě wóund,| smíliňg"); the dactylic mystery, so strong that the youth accepts it over life, prevails until the moment of his death, which occurs, of course, in iambs ("Aňd díed,| cǒntént").

One of the strangest and most revealing aspects of poem 27 is that one triple-foot figure murders another. The youth's contentment with this situation reinforces the interpretation that the triple measure is really killing itself, resigning itself or sacrificing itself to the author-ity of the iamb. In poem 10, triple feet also describe a frightening fate. Although this time the loss of the iambic norm rather than its pres-ence poses a threat to the speaker, the acceptance of doom in the company of triple feet parallels the youth's acceptance of his own death:

Should the wide world roll away,
Léavǐng blàck| térrǒr,
Límǐtlěss| níght,
Nǒr Gód,| nǒr mán,| nǒr pláce| tǒ stánd
Would be to me essential,
Íf thóu ǎnd thỳ| white arms wěre| thére,
Aňd thě fáll| tǒ dóom| ǎ lòng wáy.

The sublime dactylic abyss described in the second and third lines resembles the "mighty sky" in poem 66, which is also dactylic ("Échǒlěss,| ígnǒrǎnt"), and as in that poem, iambs present the normal, conventional human supports that oppose the abyss: "Nŏr Gód,| nŏr mán,| nŏr pláce| tŏ stánd." Here, however, the presence of a lover who shares dactylic aspects with the abyss and makes it bearable alleviates the blank, helpless fear of poem 66. Like the youth who gladly accepts his death because its "medieval fashion" enchants him, the speaker in poem 10 is able to confront nothingness in the imagined company of a sublime force described in triple feet.

These readings suggest a possible gender aspect to the metrical conflict, which is borne out by one Crane poem in particular, poem 45:

> Tră|dítiŏn,| thóu ărt fŏr| súcklĭng| chíldren,
> Thŏu| árt thĕ ĕn|lívĕnĭng| mílk fŏr| bábes;
> Bŭt| nó mĕat fŏr| mén ĭs ĭn| thée.   Bŭt nŏ mĕat| fŏr mén|
> Thĕn—̆   ĭs ĭn thée.
> Bŭt, ălás,| wĕ áll| ăre bábes.

The first two lines, some of the longest and strongest triple rhythms in *The Black Riders,* personify the abstraction "tradition" as female, reinforcing the frequent suggestion of hidden, strange, and generally "other" characteristics in Crane's triple feet. The third line metrically embodies the ambiguity of its message. It can be scanned as two anapests and an iamb, in which case one stresses "meat" and pronounces the statement as if it were a sure and defiant assertion that "tradition" cannot provide the meat the speaker is sure he needs. But it can also be scanned as dactyls, in which case one stresses "no," giving the statement a more wistful and half-questioning tone, as if the speaker might like to find something else for himself in tradition instead. The copresence of these two metrical patterns emphasizes a double message; on the one hand, there is no meat (rising meters) for men in tradition; on the other hand, maybe men are not as much men as they think they are, and maybe meat is not really what they need. (The line's metrical subtlety is even more evident since the most syntactically straightforward way to make this statement would be in dogged iambics: "There is no meat for men in thee.") The last line asserts the iambic/anapestic meter without ambiguity. If one allows the metrical code to color the line's meaning, the poem's closing statement belies its message; according to his meter, the speaker is likely to continue his rejection of dactylic tradition in spite of his apparent reconciliation with a need for it on the semantic level.

Poem 17 also associates dactyls with a kind of childishness or feminized weakness, and anapests and iambs with heroism. The first stanza describes "mány whŏ| wént ĭn| húddlĕd prŏ|céssiŏn," not knowing where they are going, but at least "sŭc|céss ŏr că|lámĭtў / Woŭld ătténd| aĺl ĭn ĕ|qúalĭtў." In contrast to the sheeplike dactyls that conclude these two lines,

> Thĕre wăs one| whŏ soúght| ă new road.
> Hĕ| wént ĭntŏ| direfuĺl| thíckĕts,
> Ănd úl|tĭmàte|lў hĕ| dièd thús,| ălóne;
> Bŭt thĕy said| hĕ hăd coúr|ăge.

This heroic "one" begins his journey in anapests, and he dies in an iambic pentameter. In between, he enters a thicket of falling rhythms. If "went into" in the second line of the stanza is scanned as a dactyl, the phrase retains a connection between the activities of this single traveler and the group he has left—a connection reaffirmed when the group finally labels him (in anapests, as if they themselves have picked some of his rising rhythm by his example) as courageous. In either case, this single "one" exhibits the same kind of dogged iambic courage against dactylic conformity as that shown by the speaker in poem 47:

> "Thínk ăs Ĭ| thínk," saĭd ă| mán,
> ŏr yóu| ăre ă|bómĭnăblў| wíckĕd;
> yóu are ă| toád."
>
> Ănd áf|tĕr Ĭ| hăd thoúght| ŏf ĭt,
> Ĭ said:| "Ĭ wíll,| thĕn, bĕ| ă toád."

With the same extra syllable that shows the pain and desperation of the man being tortured by triple feet in poem 19 ("And bit| mádlў ăt thĕ| feet of the god"), the first man in this poem reveals his own fanatical desperation ("or you are a|bómĭnăblў| wicked"). This man, however, unlike the man in poem 19, actively tries to force his ways on the speaker, and the speaker responds by asserting his resistance in two heavy, singsong iambic tetrameters.

In both this poem and poem 17, discussed above, dactyls take on a force that threatens someone's independence to the point where he chooses a bad fate rather than submission to them. In each poem, the bad fate is expressed in iambs. Since, as we have seen, iambs tend for the most part to be associated with conventional behavior in *The Black Riders,* and dactyls with more immediate and usually richer experience, the pattern in poems 17 and 19 may appear paradoxical: in each case the protagonist flees from dactyls to iambs instead of the other way around.

A gender-related model may explain this apparent paradox, in view of the complex of roughly gender-related characteristics associated with the dactyl in Crane. If we associate iambic (or, more generally, rising) rhythms with traditional patriarchal conventions, and dactylic rhythms with a feminized alternate system, Crane is caught between the two. Tending for the most part to resist the traditional iambic systems in a search for something quieter, less established, and more authentic, he still panics occasionally when faced with an overly strong dactylic rhythm, and returns to the iambic systems that can ensure him an easily comprehensible moral code and a definitely attainable heroism.

A final pair of poems from *The Black Riders* can serve to illustrate this sometimes paralyzing conflict between the sublime yet frightening connotations of triple feet and the established yet overpowering iambic connotations. Poem 20 describes an encounter between the speaker and his would-be guide:

> A lear|nĕd măn came| tŏ me once.
> He said:| "Ĭ know| thĕ way,—come.
> And Ĭ| wăs o|vĕrjoyed| ăt this.
> To|gethĕr wĕ| hastĕned.
> Soon,| tŏo soon,| wĕre we
> Where mў| eyes wĕre| usĕlĕss,
> And Ĭ knew| nŏt thĕ ways| ŏf my feet.
> Ĭ clung| tŏ thĕ hand| ŏf my friend;
> Bŭt ăt last| hĕ cried:| "Ĭ am lost."

A triple-foot pattern confidently participates in the poem's first line, but it becomes confused as the learned man begins to talk, particularly with the final imperative, "come." In strong iambs in the third line, the speaker establishes his own clear, simple point of view, very different from the learned man's rhythms. But his iambic certainty is also soon lost in a stalemate of rhythms. Triple feet recur, at first in a dactyl, when the speaker describes traveling "together" with the learned man to an unspecified place, and they continue as the speaker and the learned man become increasingly tangled in mysterious and unreliable triple feet.

If the learned man has a dactylic wisdom in the poem discussed above, it is a fragile and easily lost wisdom. In poem 63, a stronger man manages to hold on to a briefly dactylic rhythm in spite of clear iambic threats:

> Thére wăs ă| gréat că|thédrăl.
> Tŏ sól|ĕmn sóngs,
> Ă| whíte prŏ|céssiŏn
> Móved tŏward thĕ| áltăr.
> Thĕ chíef| màn thére
> Wàs ĕ|réct, ănd| bóre hĭmsélf| próudlў.
> Yĕt sóme| cŏuld sée| hĭm crínge,
> As ín ă| pláce ŏf| dánger,
> Thrówĭng| fríghtĕned| gláncĕs| íntŏ| thĕ áir,
> A-stárt| ăt thréat|ĕnĭng fác|ĕs ŏf| thĕ pást.

The procession that moves toward the altar is dactylic, suggesting that the power of this meter is not yet realized but still in process. Both the description of the chief man's pride and erectness and that of the dangerousness of the place are dactylic as well. It is clear from some of the readings above that both the pride and the danger are justified in the face of the opposing meter, the iambic pentameter that comes from the past in the last line to haunt this dactylic priest.

When Higginson wrote, in one of the first reviews of *The Black Riders,* that the book was composed of "poetry torn up by the roots" (68), he probably wasn't thinking in specifically metrical terms, but the phrase is an excellent metaphor for what occurs on a metrical level in these poems. In many of them can be found metrical roots, fragile rhythmical echoes of other poetic traditions. But these roots are not lodged and nourished in a broader metrical context as they are in the work of other nineteenth-century poets, including Whitman. They hang isolated in the blank space of the page. To many of Crane's contemporaries, such torn-up metrical language with its conflicting rhythmic impulses was not poetry at all. But insofar as Crane's poetry reflects, with courage and honesty, the stalemated poetic and prosodic traditions faced by a poet of the 1890s, it earns its place among those traditions.

Chapter 5

T. S. Eliot and the Metrical Crisis
of the Early Twentieth Century

Prosodically, T. S. Eliot has been seen as both a radical innovator and as an archconservative, as a shocking rebel and as an upholder of traditional poetic values. He might have been speaking of himself when he noted that Pound had been "hanged for a cat and drowned for a rat," labeled both an overdisciplined and a formally unstructured poet ("Ezra Pound" 48). Harvey Gross attempts to explain the confusion with the complaint that "some early and obviously deaf critics labeled Eliot a 'free-verse poet' and since first misconceptions . . . doggedly persist, many still think of Eliot as a writer of unmetered verse" (175).[1] Thorough recent analyses, however, continue to yield contradictory interpretations of Eliot's metric, suggesting that his prosody is as responsible for the situation as is historical precedent. For example, while Sister M. Martin Barry, after a book-length statistical analysis of Eliot's meters, concludes that Eliot is an accentual-syllabic poet—"his general practice is well within the limits of metrical verse" (105)—Charles Hartman defines Eliot's metric as free verse written on the same principles as that of William Carlos Williams (9). Roy Fuller, assuming that Eliot intends to write free verse, solves the problem by inventing an acronym for the apparently random metrical passages that he finds scattered throughout Eliot's poetry: UME's, or "unintended metrical effects" (45–46).[2]

The same kinds of contrasting interpretations are evident whether the topic is Eliot's prosody in general or that of his individual poems. Conrad Aiken calls "The Love Song of J. Alfred Prufrock" "rhymed free verse" (194), while Helen Gardner classifies its meter as "duple rising rhythm . . . the basic meter of our heroic line" (17). Ruth Nevo notes the "absence of obvious conventional poetic features such as meter" in *The Waste Land* (98), while David Perkins finds that the same poem uses "traditional meters in a quite irregular way" (317). Nancy K. Gish agrees that *The Waste Land* uses traditional meters, but hears them as a "predominantly iambic rhythm" (34), while Harvey Gross finds that the poem moves between strong-stress accentualism and iambic meter (187). Donald Stanford asserts that *"Four Quartets* has no formulable meter or prosody" (78), Gardner sees its norm as a four-stress line (29), Derek Stanford and Julie Whitby read it as a dynamic between verse and prose, and Harvey Gross classifies each section in terms of either iambic or strong-stress verse (207).

As might be expected from Eliot's prosody, his literary essays reflect conflicting ideas about the extent to which poetry necessarily involves meter. In "The Borderline of Prose," for instance, he concludes that "the only absolute distinction to be drawn is that poetry is written in verse, and verse is written in prose; or, in other words, that there is prose rhythm and verse rhythm" (158). Verse rhythm is an essential element in this definition of poetry. In the preface to Eliot's translation of Perse's *Anabase,* however, he suggests that poetry has no essential connection with verse rhythm: "a writer . . . is sometimes able to write poetry in what is called prose. Another writer can, by reversing the process, write great prose in verse" (64).[3] Such paradoxes in theory, like the paradoxes in practice, make sense from a poet who felt that, ideally, verse should exist in a broad area between freedom and limitation, and who defined good free verse as poetry that uses, not meter, but the "ghost" of meter ("Reflections" 34).

Within the context of early twentieth-century prosodic history, such raging paradoxes at the heart of a major poet's work are not as anomalous as they might seem. The very slipperiness that makes it hard to characterize Eliot's metrical practice today was, I would argue, a major factor in the establishment of his reputation, since such a prosody could answer to the ambivalence about free verse that arose in the wake of the free-verse revolution.[4] Writing neither free verse nor traditional verse, but deeply engaged with both, Eliot could satisfy at once the need to search for a new metrical standard and the fear of finding such a standard.

Part 1: The Free-verse Fashion in the Early Twentieth Century

The second issue of *Poetry* magazine, in November 1912, included the following item in the "Notes and Announcements" column at the back of the magazine:

> Mr. Richard Aldington is a young English member of the "Imagistes," a group of ardent Hellenists who are pursuing interesting experiments in "vers libre," trying to attain in English certain subtleties of cadence of the kind which Mallarmé and his followers have studied in French. Mr. Aldington has published little as yet, and nothing in America. (Monroe, "Notes and Announcements" 65)

The notice gives little foretaste of the extent to which vers libre would transform not only the pages of *Poetry,* but the nature and status of poetry all over America in the next two or three years. Many influences had been leading to free verse for a long time, but after they had converged, the first free-verse movement developed and declined astonishingly quickly and was astonishingly widespread. Nonmetrical verse was as common in American poetry during the beginning of the twentieth century as iambic pentameter had been in English and American poetry for the preceding three hundred and fifty years. This change fundamentally altered the nature of the metrical code in twentieth-century poetry.

A common view of the free-verse movement is that it was a "revolution," a sudden and violent eruption of reactions against long-established tendencies in poetic meter, diction, and subject matter, led by a few intrepid literary innovators. Charles Hartman's depiction of the rise of free verse is representative. He sets the scene for the birth of free verse with the remark, "In 1908 the world was in order" (3). At that time, he continues, there was no question that "verse was composed of metrical feet. . . . The debates [concerning prosody] were the refinements of experts" (4). In the usual model, this settled prosodic world is suddenly interrupted by the entrance of one or more heroic radicals who forcefully instigate a drastic prosodic change. Hartman's description continues, "by 1912 . . . Pound would formulate Imagism. He would command the young poet . . . 'to compose in the sequence of the musical phrase, not in sequence of a metronome'" (5). This development was so sudden that "the break with the prosodic past seemed as great as the First World War's destruction of historical certainties and modern literature's denial of all that had come before" (8).

An analysis such as Hartman's rests on the work of traditional theorists of accentual-syllabic prosody, such as T. S. Omond and George Saintsbury, who did not anticipate the free-verse movement. But the lack of theoretical discussion of free-verse prosody before 1912 does not mean that free verse developed suddenly or unexpectedly. Many signs of free verse were evident among American poets and literary critics earlier in the century. Among the poets who began to abandon meter well before Pound's pronouncement are Vachel Lindsay, who went on his first walking tour to perform Whitman-influenced poetry in 1906; Edward Lee Masters, who began writing the free-verse *Spoon River Anthology* in 1909; and H.D., who had been writing in free verse for some time by 1911 (Stauffer 242, 245, 275). Pound himself seems to have learned about the French symbolist use of free verse from T. E. Hulme, who founded the Poets' Club in London in 1908 in order to read and discuss free-verse and imagist poems, including his own. When Pound first showed up at the Poets' Club in April 1909, he had just published a prosodically traditional book and had not yet discovered free verse; he was, in the words of F. S. Flint, still "very full of his troubadours" (qtd. in Hughes 10–12).

The roots of these various manifestations of free verse were clearly evident in the late nineteenth century.[5] Experiments with idiomatic speech rhythms by prosodic traditionalists such as Hardy, Robinson, and Frost, all of whom were writing poetry in the 1890s, were already leading towards new ideas of poetic cadence. Critics began formulating broader definitions of poetic rhythm as a result of the growing acceptance of Whitman's poetry,[6] and Whitman's direct influence on some poets of the 1890s evolved into the idiom of Lindsay and Sandburg. Though Whitman did not have his most widespread impact on free verse until the 1950s, his influence was strong enough on the early modernist poets for William Carlos Williams to write, in the "Prologue" to his *Selected Essays,* that "modern poetry, what there was of it, and especially the free verse of Walt Whitman, opened my eyes" (ii).

A significant part of Whitman's influence on American free verse came by way of French poets. In the November 1912 issue of *Poetry*, associate editor Alice Corbin Henderson discusses the remarkable importance of Whitman in Europe and lists a number of young French poets who have been inspired by Whitman. She notes that

> there have been more followers of the Whitman method in Europe than in America. . . . The rhythmic measure of Whitman has yet to be correctly estimated by English and American poets. It has been sifted and weighed by the French poets, and though Whitman's influence upon modern French poetry has been questioned by English critics, the connection between his varied rhythmic units and modern *vers libre* is too obvious to be discounted. ("A Perfect Return" 90–91)

Stephen Crane's poems, prosodically more similar than Whitman's to vers libre, had a more immediate and direct, although often undiscussed, influence on American free verse. Horace Gregory names Crane as one of the handful of "true forerunners" of American modernist poetry, noting that the introduction to the 1925 edition of Crane's collected works was by Amy Lowell (58). Perhaps because Crane was not nearly as much of a self-proclaimed poet as was Whitman, his influence seems to have been more easily and more unobtrusively accepted than Whitman's. While Pound and Eliot both wrote passionately about their love/hate relationship with Whitman as a type of threatening father figure, Crane's style simply appears, without fanfare, in early twentieth-century poems. The very first proto-imagist poems by Hulme, for instance, remarkably resemble Crane's in tone and cadence. This is "Autumn":

> A touch of cold in the Autumn night—
> I walked abroad,
> And saw the ruddy moon lean over a hedge
> Like a red-faced farmer.
> I did not stop to speak, but nodded,
> And round about were the wistful stars
> With white faces like town children. (qtd. in Hughes 18)

The widespread tendency to free verse in the very first years of the twentieth century is evident not only in the poetry being written, but in the opinions being voiced in scholarly journals. As early as

1902, Charles Leonard Moore's essay on "The Lost Art of Blank Verse" reveals a significant lack of faith in meter. In the absence of rhyme, quantity, and strict syllable count in blank verse, argues Moore, "the only legal hold on form is the slight stress or halt at the end of the tenth syllable" (319). Moore's apparent inability to *hear* meter on its own belies his claim that meter is "the one solid distinction between poetry and prose"; he does not grant meter the status of a "legal hold" on form (319). Other scholars continued to argue, as had Arthur Clive in 1875, that prose is simply a superior literary form to verse.[6] D. Winter, writing in the *Journal of English and Germanic Philology* in 1903, already sounds like a modernist in his privileging of prose rhythms over meter: prose rhythms are "far more complex than verse-rhythms" (284), and "prose is a freer and more natural medium than verse, but for this very reason it is also a more difficult medium, as well as a nobler medium. . . . Only great souls are fit for freedom" (285).

At the same time, critics were loosening the definition of verse itself in scholarly journals. Fred Newton Scott argued in *PMLA* in 1904 that the definitive characteristic of poetry in relation to prose is its expressive as opposed to communicative function. Scott calls this distinction far more "fundamental" than the traditional rhythmic one (263). In the *English Review* in 1911, two years before Pound published his assault on poems written in the "sequence of the metronome," John Robertson attacked overly regular meter and dubbed it "pedal meter." Robertson asserted that great poetry must be "rhythmically perfect," even if that meant that it has to be "metrically indescribable" (387).

In spite of the various influences tending towards free verse in the early century in America, it is still no accident that the first term used for the new movement in English was the French phrase *vers libre*. In fact, America's most well-known published statement on free verse was intimately related to a French text. One of the first three imagist tenets that, according to Pound, was "agreed upon" by H.D., Aldington, and himself in 1912 states: "As regarding rhythm, to compose in the sequence of the musical phrase, not in sequence of a metronome" ("Retrospect" 3). Harvey Gross points out how closely the aphoristic form and phrasing of the imagist tenets resembles that of "Notes sur la technique poetique," the treatise on vers libre that Georges Duhamel and Charles Vildrac published in France in 1910. Duhamel and Vildrac supplied the imagists with their most famous prosodic metaphor in the phrase, "nous pouvons chanter sans metronome" (Gross 102).

To some extent the influence of French poetry on Eliot and Pound, including their adoption of the term vers libre and the revolutionary stance of the vers librists, was the conscious and direct result of reading French poets and poetic theory. Pound was influenced, largely through Hulme, by Gautier, Rimbaud, Corbière, and Laforgue. Eliot credited Jules Laforgue as the crucial initial influence on his poetic style, calling him in an early talk "the first to teach me how to speak" ("Talk on Dante" 107). Years later Eliot remarked, "My early vers libre, of course, was started under the endeavor to practice the same form as Laforgue. This meant merely rhyming lines of irregular length" ("Art of Poetry" 55).[7] But perhaps Pound and Eliot's familiarity with a language whose traditional prosody, a purely syllabic one, is so radically different from English was ultimately a more significant factor in the birth of free verse. C. K. Stead postulates that Eliot's extensive training in French literature was essential to freeing his ear from conventional English meters:[8]

> It is easy to *decide* to break out of the traditional form; but to do so effectively the ear must be reeducated—and it is likely that Eliot achieved this by submerging himself so thoroughly in the French language and in French poetry that he was able after a time to return to English liberated. (49)

Since accent plays no significant role in French prosody, contact with French poetry probably accelerated the tendency to override accentual syllabism already begun with the nineteenth-century cultivation of triple rhythms in English.[9] Modernist poets, already caught between two different metrical systems in their own language, were ripe to lose or abandon any English accentual pattern in favor of nonaccentual cadences on the model of vers libre. Pound mentioned the influence of still another metrical system—a system long associated with triple meters in English—when he speculated that syllable quantity was more important in free than in metered verse: "the desire for vers libre is due to the sense of quantity reasserting itself after years of starvation" ("Retrospect" 12). He may have been thinking of the fact that H.D. and Richard Aldington, as well as Edgar Lee

Masters, were inspired to write free verse by their readings in classical Greek poetry.[10]

All of this impetus to write in free verse, whether in America or in Europe, would not have resulted in the free-verse movement had it not been for a more subtle, and perhaps even more compelling cause: the connotations that metrical verse, and iambic pentameter in particular, had been building throughout the nineteenth century. That Dickinson, Whitman, and Crane were disillusioned with the pentameter is evident in metrical-code readings of their work. The association of meter with constraint and rigidity became more and more common among poets by the turn of the century.

One widespread aspect of nineteenth-century poetry that aggravated its metrical rigidity and increased the modernists' frustration with meter was the habit of reading poetry aloud with an unnatural emphasis on the underlying metrical pattern. An editorial in the 1912 inaugural issue of *Poetry* offers the following scenario as a partial explanation for the lack of popular respect for poetry:

> People achieve the deadly habit of reading metrical lines unimaginatively. After forming—generally in preparation for entering one of our great universities—the habit of blinding the inner eye, deafening the inner ear, and dropping into a species of mental coma before a page of short lines, it is difficult for educated persons to read poetry with what is is known as "ordinary human intelligence." (Monroe, "On the Reading" 23–24)

Timothy Steele, who writes about this phenomenon in *Missing Measures (59–65)*, discusses the prestige of prose, the model of scientific progress, and the legacy of the romantic notion of organic form as other factors in the rise of free verse. In addition, Steele revises the usual account of the most familiar cause of the free-verse movement: a rebellion against the elaborate music of late-nineteenth-century metrical virtuosos such as Swinburne and Tennyson. While conceding that "metrical composition accommodates [inflated diction] more readily than prose," Steele argues that the modernist rejection of meter itself was based on an unnecessary confusion of meter with an artificial poetic idiom:

With the best of motives and intentions, [the leaders of the modernist revolution] objected to the diction and attendant subject matter of Victorian verse. Yet they identified Victorian poetry with the metrical system which the Victorians used but which was not in itself Victorian, having been used for centuries by a variety of poets working in a variety of styles...such an identification confuses properties which have been recognized as distinguishable for most of literary history. (34–35)

In support of his claim that the modernists confused meter with diction, Steele notes that Pound and Eliot consistently emphasized unaffected writing, not adherence to free-verse principles, as the key to the new poetry (42). The free-verse mode simply accompanied the cleaning up of poetic language. William Carlos Williams equates archaic poetic diction with the line itself in a letter to Kay Boyle: "There can no longer be serious work in poetry written in 'poetic' diction. It is a contortion of speech to conform to a rigidity of line" ("Letter" 269). Steele notes that Williams, writing of the poetry of Byron Vazakas, found fault with regular meter as "the line in which the worst cliches of the art of poetry lie anchored" (43). Steele also quotes Ford Madox Ford's description of the poetry readings by Robert Browning, Tennyson, and the Rossettis that he heard as a child: "It went on and on—and on! A long, rolling stream of words which no-one would ever use, to endless monotonous, polysyllabic, unchanging rhythms" (qtd. in Steele 38). Such identification of rhythms with the words in them, of course, is the cause of the association of specific rhythms with specific ideas that is revealed by the metrical code. At the beginning of the modernist movement, however, the distinctions between the connotations of various meters were lost in the general movement against meter.

Summing up his satisfaction with the imagist movement in 1921, Ford notes with relief that imagism avoids "the polysyllabic, honey-dripping and derivative adjectives that . . . makes [sic] nineteenth-century poetry as a whole seem greasy and 'close,' like the air of a room" (qtd. in Steele 39). This allusion to "the air of a room" brings out another, less generally recognized aspect of the modernist turn to free verse: the association of regular meter with a sentimental, domestic, feminized poetic tradition. Some of the most successful poets of the late nineteenth century had been women such as Ella Wheeler Wilcox and Louise Imogen Guiney. Continuing the "sentimental" aesthetic of midcentury poetesses including Lydia Sigourney and Frances Osgood, the women poets of the 1890s had transformed the pious religious and nature poetry of their predecessors into a popular tradition that explored the emotional life of the "new woman" in regular verse forms. In the early twentieth century, this female poetic tradition continued with the work of such poets as Sara Teasdale and Edna St. Vincent Millay, who continued to write in traditional poetic form even after the modernist revolt. Male modernist poets could draw strength from a long history of poetic and prosodic revolutions, but, as Suzanne Clark has pointed out, women's poetry tended to value accessibility and the building of community over radical innovation. In Clark's view, women poets in the modernist period were caught in a double bind. The price of participation in the new movements was the abandonment of the whole female poetic tradition: "a modern woman poet could not be a woman poet without reaching for a tradition that would violate the unconventionality of modernism and seem politically regressive" (145).

At various points, almost all the major male modernists made clearly evident their contempt for the female tradition in poetry and their relief at having so definitively broken with it. Pound remarked that he had always wanted "to write 'poetry' that a grown man could read without groans of ennui, or without having to have it cooed in his ear by a flapper" (qtd. in Perkins 298). Sandra Gilbert and Susan Gubar's study of women writers in the twentieth century, *No Man's Land,* collects a number of other such remarks, including James Joyce's comment, on his first reading of *The Waste Land,* that it "ends [the] idea of poetry for ladies"; William Carlos Williams's verse, "Of sugar and spice and everything nice, / That is what bad poetry is made of" (155); and Pound's claim that "poetry speaks phallic direction" (156).

Though their contempt for the women who wrote in the conservative female poetic tradition is less clearly expressed than that of the male modernists, some of the women who participated in the modernist movement shared the same opinion. H.D.'s biographer Barbara Guest remarks that "privately, [H.D.] considered herself and

[Marianne] Moore far superior to other women poets such as Elinor Wylie, Edna St. Vincent Millay, or Sara Teasdale" (133). Amy Lowell discusses H.D. but not Teasdale in her *Tendencies in Modern American Poetry,* and even Harriet Monroe, who included enthusiastic essays on Teasdale, Millay, and Wylie as well as on H.D. and Lowell in her collection, *Poets and Their Art,* reveals a bias for male poetry in a 1920 editorial in *Poetry.* Writing to defend the magazine against the charge that it is female dominated, Monroe notes that twice as many pages are filled with men's poetry as with women's and continues, *"Poetry* receives more publishable verse, and less hopelessly bad verse, from the 'vigorous male' than from the aspiring female." The associate editor corroborates: "more rotten verse comes from women than from men" (Monroe, "Men or Women?" 148).

As Anita Sokolsky points out, sentimentality and modernism are fundamentally opposed:

> From modernism on, forswearing sentimentality has been a reflex gesture of literary good faith. . . . Such exhaustive ease, the result of an apparent naivete about the relation of expression to meaning, forms an affront to a generation of writers and readers for whom difficulty was an ethos. (68)

The fact that women's poetry was associated with sentimentality, and sentimentality with formal verse, meant that the full force of the modernist revolution—both its misogyny and its hatred of the traditional and bourgeois—was brought to bear on the crafted female lyric. The strength of the initial rejection can be guessed from the momentum it maintained even among women poets throughout the rest of the century; Anne Sexton—in spite of a secret love for Millay and Teasdale (Middlebrook 196)—complained in 1959 that "I didn't know a damn thing about any poetry really. 2 years ago I had never heard of any poet but Edna St. Vincent," suggesting that Millay's poetry has nothing to teach about what is "really" poetry (79). Gilbert and Gubar analyze women writers' rejection of their poetic predecessors at length in *No Man's Land,* citing Virginia Woolf's "hatchet job" on Ella Wheeler Wilcox in "Wilcoxiana" and Sylvia Plath's "determination not to be 'quailing or whining like Teasdale or [to write] simple lyrics like Millay' " (204, 206). The fact that Gilbert and Gubar themselves omit Teasdale from their 1985 *Norton Anthology of Literature by Women* provides further evidence that the bias against the mainstream female poetic tradition continues to this day.

In view of all the intersecting pressures against formal verse during the first two decades of the century, the free-verse movement is not surprising. It is more surprising that any poet who used meter could become a highly influential figure in the first half of the century. T. S. Eliot built his formidable reputation as the representative poet of his generation with a prosody that is not clearly free verse at all. To understand the success of Eliot's prosody, the subject of the second part of this chapter, it is crucial to recognize that the early free-verse movement bore many of the distinguishing marks of a fad. His metrics answered the needs of a literary public that had adopted free verse quickly and tired of it just as quickly.

J. Isaacs, who calls the years from 1912 to 1922 the "Great Poetry Boom," estimates that an unprecedented one thousand poets published more than two thousand volumes during the first ten years of free verse (37). The extent to which the fashion had caught on is evident in the fact that within two years after the publication of the first imagist call for free verse, schools were encouraging students to write it. Horace Gregory gives Amy Lowell credit for the trend of free verse written by children that began around 1915:

> Her spontaneously written verses encouraged school girls to write millions of impressionistic fragments for the delight of their school teachers and startled yet happy parents. . . . During the following ten years in America, the "freedom" of Amy Lowell's verse led to the discovery of many girl prodigies. In grade schools throughout the United States something like a children's crusade for "free verse" took fire. . . . In New York, teachers and magazine editors—even publishers—flamed their fancies with verses written or dictated by children who could scarcely read. (144)

When the textbook on versification for the Home Correspondence School saw fit to add a chapter on vers libre to the 1916 edition, it opened with the remark that "this new style seems formless" but added the justifying observation, "It has been taken up with enthusiasm, and hundreds of people in England and America are now writing poems in unrhymed lines of unequal length" (Esenwein, Berg, and Roberts 298). Joyce Kilmer reported that between 1915 and 1917 the short story writers' club at Columbia University had disappeared, to be replaced by a club devoted to reading poetry and publishing a poetry journal (206). In a May 1916 editorial in *Poetry*—for several years the only periodical in America devoted to poetry—Harriet Monroe summed up what had happened in the previous three years:

> In January, 1913, the art was still in the old era . . . and the public was serenely indifferent. Now all is changed. It is as though some magician had waved his wand—presto, the beggar is robed in scarlet. Indeed, the present danger may be that poetry is becoming the fashion. ("Down East" 85)

Monroe notes that poetry has moved from the dark back corners of urban bookstores to "the foremost table," where crowds of people now jostle each other to buy it. The change is also evident in the emergence of new poetry magazines—"Is it possible that only three and a half brief years ago we were alone in the field?" she asks—and of poets themselves, who "seem as numerous as sparrows through the cool spring sunshine, and almost as quarrelsome" ("Down East" 86–87). A month later, already beginning to sound perhaps a little weary, she reported, "Never before was there so much talk about poetry in this western world, or so much precious print devoted to its schools and schisms" ("Various Views" 140).[11]

But all this enthusiasm for free verse was short-lived, and the "poetry boom" itself would not outlast it for long. By the time Eliot's first book was published, the literary world was becoming disillusioned with both imagism and the free verse associated with it. Monroe's fear that the new popularity of poetry was "a real danger, because the poets need an audience, not fitful and superficial, but loyal and sincere," turned out to be justified ("Down East" 85). In 1915, Monroe reiterated the imagist objections to meter—

> Certain metric forms and rhyme tunes have been followed by so many generations of English poets that the modern world has come to think them fundamental. . . . And these forms and tunes have been covered over with ornaments and excrescences. ("Its Inner Meaning" 304)

But the same issue of *Poetry* carried a letter from Floyd Dell indicating that he already found the new aesthetic as limiting as the old: "Whenever I find a poem that seems beautiful to me, I want to quarrel with everybody who would deny its beauty either on the ground that it is 'not poetry' or that it is 'too old-fashioned'" (319). In the same issue, a parodic free-verse poem by Allen Upward remarked, "I hear that already Imagism is out of date" (318).

In 1915 the poet Arthur Davison Ficke wrote in *The Dial* that "unrhymed cadence at its best can hardly convey that intensity of effect which is poetry's peculiar function" (12). His opinion is not surprising, since he himself was continuing to write in form. Edward Storer, on the other hand, may have been one of the first practicing free-verse poets to imply that he felt his own poetry was confined by participation in a movement officially only three years old. Storer's opinion, expressed in the *New Republic* in March 1916, does much to explain the subsequent fading of the free-verse fashion. "Free verse is no longer an experiment, no longer even a new movement," the essay begins. Storer continues,

> At the same time one is aware of a certain feeling of dissatisfaction with regard to it and its limitations. We use it because we must, because it is more real than conventional metres. . . . A poet who wishes to give expression to realities in modern life . . . will find in practice that he is confined for his literary expression to the two media of prose and free verse. (154)

Storer's essay maintains that traditional forms are no longer viable for serious poetry because our culture has lost the religious impulse that should underlie rhythmic utterance. But phrasing such as "we use it because we must" and "he is confined" indicates that he is dissatisfied with the situation. At one point, he defines free verse as an undeveloped substitute for metrical poetry: "Free verse is verse true in material and inspiration, which has not succeeded in obtaining for itself a definite form. It is a literary expression which has failed to take its most convenient and final shape" (154).

In the same journal several months later, Max Eastman attacked free verse, from without, with fewer qualms. Eastman compares "the new dilute variety of prosy poetry which is watering the country" to journalism; he charges that irregular line breaks are a cheap bid for the reader's attention, like "display-advertising" (138–39).[12] In *Poetry* magazine's response to Eastman's assault, Alice Corbin Henderson reveals her own dissatisfaction with the stylistic course free verse has taken before entering into her defense of free verse: "we sympathize with Mr. Eastman. . . . It is high time that a critic objected to vers libre, not on the score of rhythm—a phase of the subject endlessly debatable, but on the score of style" ("Lazy Criticism" 144).

Between 1916 and 1918 the essays in *Poetry* continue to maintain, as they had from the beginning, that free and traditional verse can both be appropriate options for different poems; yet they show a new disillusionment with the dogmatic dominance of free verse as a literary movement. Harriet Monroe remarks that Alfred Kreymborg's "'free forms' are not always so good a fit for the serious as for the whimsical mood; their rhythms become as obvious in their way as certain familiar hymns are in theirs" ("Staccato" 53). In another issue she mentions that "hundreds of outpourings of chopped prose, quite innocent of poetic cadence, arrive at this office every month" ("Dr. Patterson" 35).

In 1919, *Poetry* published its first full-scale critique of free verse, Henderson's "Mannerisms of Free Verse." Henderson writes of "the pompous solemnity of [free verse's] platitudes, which, broken into fragments, would seem to the author to be less bromidically obvious than if stated in plain prose." She also notes that "there is such a marked similarity among free verse practitioners today that without a signature it is difficult to tell one from another" (95–97). In a reply in the next issue, Maxwell Bodenheim complains that free verse has come disproportionately under attack: "those who belabor mediocrity in free verse have only a passing mention for the triteness and futility of average rhymed and metrical poetry. Why is all the emphasis placed upon one side of the question?" (173).

A possible explanation for the prejudice Bodenheim had noticed—resentment of free-verse propaganda—was suggested the following year by Llewellyn Jones in the *Sewanee Review:* "perhaps the salient thing about the free verse movement, however, is not its actual achievement . . . but it is the intense propaganda promoted by the free verse writers for their particular methods" (384). In a review, Henderson summarizes what seems to have been a prevailing mood in 1919, three years before the publication of *The Waste Land:*

> In the last few years so much has been written in defense of
> radicalism in poetry, so much has been said of the hampering
> restrictions of what has been regarded as conventional, conserva-
> tive verse, that now perhaps it becomes necessary to defend the
> classics against what we may call the "new Academicism"—of
> the radicals! ("Convention and Revolt" 269)

When Harriet Monroe stated her belief during the same year
"that more, rather than less, freedom of form is coming," she could
not have been more wrong, judging from what transpired shortly in
Poetry ("What Next?" 33). The 1923 volume is full of verse in form
and talk about the return to traditional forms. Jessica North's mourn-
ful piece on "The Late Rebellion," "by one of its pallbearers," is
unequivocal: "That the present trend is away from unrhymed and
unmetrical verse cannot be denied" (155). A review of *The Principles
of English Versification* a month later notes that the book is published
"at a fortunate time, when many poets are turning away from the
newer, and freer, to the older, and more traditional, forms"
(O'Conor 220). And, in view of the "tendency recently among even
the most radical poets to return to the old forms," the entire Septem-
ber 1923 issue of *Poetry* was devoted to sonnets, including ones by
free verse writers Edgar Lee Masters, Alfred Kreymborg, Arthur
Davison Ficke, and Maxwell Bodenheim (Monroe, "Notes" 347).
Even John Gould Fletcher, one of the very first imagists, returned to
traditional form in 1921 (Stauffer 280).
   Some of the major free-verse poets themselves also began to
become disillusioned with free verse by the end of the 1910s. Eliot
wrote with a trace of disgust in 1917, "It is now possible to print free
verse (second, third, or tenth-rate) in almost any American maga-
zine" ("Ezra Pound" 40). The following year, Pound remarked that
"it is too late to prevent vers libre. But, conceivably, one might
improve it, and one might stop at least a little of the idiotic and
narrow discussion" ("Vers Libre" 437). Although Williams and Eliot
had such different prosodies, and although Williams was vehement
in his objection to what he called Eliot's "forced timing of verse after
antique patterns" ("Letter" 271), both poets were to object equally
to free verse in their later writings. Williams noted in 1932 that "for
myself, I have written little poetry lately. Form, the form has been

lacking," and continued, "there is no workable poetic form extant among us today. Free verse—if it ever existed—is out" ("Letter" 265, 270). Beginning with "Reflections on Vers Libre" in 1917, Eliot repeatedly expressed his belief that "there is no escape from metre; there is only mastery" (35); in his second Milton lecture, for instance, he reminded his listeners that "a monotony of unscannable verse fatigues the attention even more quickly than a monotony of exact feet" (274).[13]

Both Williams and Eliot, in fact, believed that free verse was not a true poetic form but an intermediate step before the creation of new forms. In 1932, Williams referred to the previous ten years as "a formless interim," and spoke hopefully of "whatever form we create during the next ten years" ("Letter" 265). Looking back on the history of free verse in 1942, Eliot expressed an identical view in "The Music of Poetry": "only a bad poet could welcome free verse as a liberation from form. It was a revolt against dead form, and a preparation for new form or for the renewal of the old" (31).

At the beginning of the period of disillusionment in 1917, Eliot and Pound decided to instigate a counter influence to free verse. They made a famous decision, described later by Pound in *The Criterion:*

> two authors, neither engaged in picking the other's pockets, decided that the dilutation of vers libre, Amygism, Lee Masterism, general floppiness had gone too far and that a counter-current must be set going. Remedy prescribed. . . . Rhyme and regular strophes. ("Harold Monro" 590)

The end results of the remedy, according to Pound, were the poems in Eliot's second volume, *Poems,* and Pound's "Mauberly." After the "counter-current" was over, Pound, like Williams and H.D., would continue to search for a viable new metric—Williams through the concept of the "variable foot," Pound through the method of ideogrammatic juxtaposition, and H.D. through free-verse couplets and complex open forms. Eliot, however, though ceasing to write in the tight quatrains of *Poems,* remained consciously involved with the tradition of metrical verse in English. Throughout his writing career, he responded to, and developed, the same kinds of prosodic tensions and connotations that had engaged Dickinson, Whitman, and Crane.

Part 2: T. S. Eliot and the Ghosts of Meter

Eliot's historical position at the edge of the free-verse movement and
his own ambivalence about the relation between poetry and verse
give his use of meter a self-awareness not possible for nineteenth-
century poets. Several critics have commented on his apparent self-
conscious use of "verse" as an aspect of poetic meaning. Hartman
postulates that Eliot manipulates our recognition of meter more than
he manipulates the meter itself (119). John Chalker describes the occa-
sional "ironic incongruity" between Eliot's meter and his content
(84), and in Erik Svarny's view, the metrical regularity at the end of
"Prufrock" "enacts a sad parody of poetic meaning" (55). Northrop
Frye offers a related observation in reference to the same poem: "the
tumbling down of wistful reverie into preoccupation is represented
by an artful sinking from 'poetry' into 'verse'" (*T. S. Eliot* 36). Louis
Menand's more general speculation about Eliot's self-conscious allu-
sive technique is also relevant to his metrical practice:

> Few poets can have mistrusted their own feelings as thoroughly
> as Eliot seems to have mistrusted his in the poetry he wrote
> before his religious conversion, and the strategy of putting feel-
> ings he suspected of being factitious in the literary quotation
> marks of imitation and allusion was one of the methods he dis-
> covered for neutralizing that mistrust. (16–17)

Regardless of how consciously Eliot manipulated the meter in
his poems, certain of his critical theories indicate that he was closer
to a conscious awareness of the metrical code than previous poets.
One such theory is that, as Austin Warren sums it up, "the meaning
of poetry is partly in its rhythm" (292). While versions of this idea
go back to the Greeks and probably earlier, Eliot develops it with a
literalness that was only possible given his historical distance from
meter and the total accessibility of free verse. In "The Music of Po-
etry" and *The Use of Poetry,* Eliot explains the quasi-semantic
significance of "the feeling for syllable and rhythm, penetrating far
below the conscious levels of thought" (*Use* 50). The well-known
statement that "a poem, or a passage of a poem, may tend to realize
itself first as a particular rhythm before it reaches expression in
words, and ... this rhythm may bring to birth the idea and the im-

age" offers a precise explanation of why certain passages of poetry can be read in terms of the metrical code ("Music" 32).

Eliot explores ideas fundamental to another aspect of the metrical code, the way in which meters can signify, in the following, almost mystical, sentences of his essay on Swinburne: "what [Swinburne] gives is not images and ideas and music, it is one thing with a curious mixture of suggestions of all three" ("Swinburne" 282); "the object [in Swinburne] has ceased to exist, because the meaning is merely the hallucination of meaning" (285). The phrase "hallucination of meaning" aptly describes the oddly self-referential signification characteristic of lines in the metrical code. Harry T. Antrim reads such passages as evidence that Eliot found "a blending of subject and object [that] exists in its own right" in Swinburne's sound patterns (32).

Whether or not Eliot consciously considered his poems in terms of metrical self-referentiality, on the metrical-code level they are dramatic. They test and explore metrical connotations constantly in their efforts to identify a tenable metrical standard. The pentameter in "The Love Song of J. Alfred Prufrock" and the pentameter and dactylic rhythms in *The Waste Land* and *Four Quartets* are manipulated through numerous stages until each poem reaches its final metrical resolution. J. Hillis Miller writes that, in Eliot's idea of language, "everything has already been named. Language may therefore be taken completely for granted" (161). The same may be said of Eliot's sense of the iambic pentameter and, to some extent, of the dactylic rhythm. These meters have already been developed and have already acquired an identity; that is why they are able to withstand the prosodic searching to which his poems subject them. Eliot's poems take these meters for granted by using metrical connotations that develop the connotations of the nineteenth century. Miller claims that Eliot's sense of language relieves him of any "anguished doubt of the validity of language" (161), and one might expect that his certainty about meter would lead to a similar result. Instead, however, Eliot's sense of established meters leads his poems into much doubt and confusion as he struggles to find a modernist voice connected with the old meters but independent of them. On one level, the desire to explore and resolve such doubt propels Eliot's poems.

Conrad Aiken writes of "The Love Song of J. Alfred Prufrock" that "in its wonderfully varied use of rhymed free verse there [is] a probable solution of the quarrel . . . about the usefulness of rhyme or

verse at all" (194). "Prufrock" can be read as a debate over the neces-
sity and value of iambic pentameter. At the time Eliot published the
poem, the prosodic debate about the possibility of classical triple
meters in English had been largely displaced by the excitement and
discussion over vers libre. Iambic pentameter was threatened much
more extremely than it had been in the time of Whitman and Crane.
Eliot's earlier poetry reflects this situation. On a metrical-code level,
"Prufrock" (first published in 1915) primarily involves the viability
of iambic pentameter. *The Waste Land* (1922) begins to explore the
implications of dactylic rhythms, and it is not until *Four Quartets*
(1942) that Eliot's poetry extensively treats both iambic pentameter
and dactylic rhythms.

"The Love Song of J. Alfred Prufrock"

At the opening of "Prufrock," meter sets up an opposition between
an independent self-consciousness, embodied in neutral prose
rhythms or nonpentameter iambic meters, and a more self-con-
sciously "poetic" realm, embodied in iambic pentameter:

> Let us go then, you and I,
> When the evening is spread out against the sky
> Like a patient etherised upon a table;
> Let us go, through certain half-deserted streets . . .

After the first, each line above is a regular pentameter with an initial
trisyllabic substitution. Because it is followed by this rush of pen-
tameters, the opening invitation, "Let us go," invites the reader into
iambic pentameter as well as into the world described in the poem.
But before long the invitation turns sour, and the poem pulls abruptly
out of the general pentameter pattern:

> Streets that follow like a tedious argument
> Of insidious intent
> To lead you to an overwhelming question . . .
> Oh, do not ask, "What is it?"
> Let us go and make our visit.

The first line of this passage could stand as a pentameter (with an
extra initial syllable and a trisyllabic substitution in the fourth foot)

in a blank-verse poem. Maintaining the meter to that extent, how-
ever, would be not only "tedious" but "insidious," according to the
meaning of these lines. To insist on keeping the poem metrical would
force the poem to confront "an overwhelming question." The meter
of this passage indicates that the metrical subject of this "question" is
the iambic pentameter.

The final, strong pentameter line is made even more insistently
metrical because the line includes the four-syllable word "over-
whelming," the longest word in any pentameter line in the poem so
far. The word straddles the last three feet of the line, making the
metrical pattern particularly strong and the meter particularly "over-
whelming," at this point. The preceding pentameters have led to this
line as the streets lead to the "overwhelming question," and the meter
draws back from the pentameter into a tetrameter couplet just as the
speaker of the poem draws back from the question with the dis-
claimer, "Oh, do not ask, 'What is it?'" The two other references to
a question in the poem also occur in pentameters, further indicating
that the "overwhelming question," which is never asked explicitly in
the poem, is significant on a metrical-code level. In terms of the
metrical code, the "question" involves the extent to which iambic
pentameter is still the only truly viable metric for ambitious poetry,
and the nature of the risks involved in either adopting or rejecting it.

With Eliot, the desires revealed by the metrical code have shifted
since the nineteenth century. Dickinson's and Whitman's major met-
rical consideration was usually how to avoid iambic pentameter, and
Crane's was to mirror the conflicting metrical forces of his time. For
all these poets, the canonical meter was there to fall back on if they
wished. Iambic pentameter is available when Dickinson wants to
evoke "awe," as in poem 1677, or when Whitman wants to establish
his poetic authority at the beginning of a poem. Even Crane, as in
poem 66, can turn to iambs to express human communality. But
Eliot was writing poetry in a different poetic world, a world in which
free verse was almost as widespread as metered verse had been at the
time of his predecessors. "Prufrock" was written not long before
John Gould Fletcher, in 1915, could matter-of-factly and in passing
drop the phrase "the break-up of blank verse": "[Amy Lowell] was
faced at the outset by the fact that the English language, since the
break-up of blank verse, has no form which is standard, like the
French alexandrine" (34).[14]

The metrical-code connotations of both Eliot's pentameters and his dactyls show a clear continuity with the practice of his nineteenth-century predecessors, but his general metrical concerns are opposite from theirs. Sean Lucy's observation on Eliot's literary theory applies equally well to his metrics: "Eliot's attitude to the conscious cultivation of a sense of tradition is an indication of a state of emergency" (18). Faced with a metrical void instead of with the titanic metrical tradition that had threatened his predecessors, Eliot is more concerned with trying to reestablish a meter than with avoiding one. The "overwhelming question" in "Prufrock," for instance, is more concerned with a new desire to adopt the pentameter than with the old desire to avoid it, in spite of a certain amount of ambivalence towards the meter.

"Prufrock's" response to the overwhelming question is, metrically, a retreat into several irregular lines. But the apparent temptation to pentameter overtakes the poem once again at the word "lingered," and the meter recurs in alternate lines through the rest of the "fog" passage:

> Lingered upon the pools that stand in drains,
> Let fall upon its back the soot that falls from chimneys,
> Slipped by the terrace, made a sudden leap,
> And seeing that it was a soft October night,
> Curled once about the house, and fell asleep.
>
> And indeed there will be time
> For the yellow smoke that slides along the street.

The pentameters in alternate lines after the word "lingered" open with trochaic substitutions, but the passage's concluding pentameter line is absolutely regular. It resolves the preparation for sleep—the lingering and leaping—with the act of falling asleep, and it resolves the previous pentameters by completely adopting the underlying metrical pattern. The whole next (fourth) stanza, one of the most regular in the poem, is full of pentameters.[15]

As if to reinforce the safety of slipping into the canonical meter, repeated nonpentameter assertions that "there will be time" punctuate the fourth stanza. Like the initial "Let us go then, you and I," these lines use the authority of free verse in order to reassure reader and poem that the pentameter is poetically acceptable. Such lines of *meta-*

free verse function for the twentieth century much as Whitman's metapentameters did for the nineteenth. The authority of the free verse is less reliable for Eliot than the authority of the pentameter was for Whitman, and Eliot uses his metaprosody less consistently than does Whitman.[16]

The lines of meta–free verse cannot keep the poem asleep in its iambic pentameter. In the middle of the fourth stanza, the "question" returns like a disturbing dream that echoes the previous question: "and time for all the works and days of hands / That lift and drop a question on your plate." As if this question had disturbed the pentameter, the poem wakes back up to free verse a few lines later. The free-verse stanza, full of self-doubt, centers on the question, "do I dare?" The first question explicitly posed in the poem, it evokes all of the previous, unasked pentameter questions. The metrical context of the passage—it is an interlude of free-verse self-consciousness between two pentameter passages—also questions the validity of pentameter as the poem here asks, "Do I dare to fall into that meter?"

After one more reassurance that "there is time" (as if "time" referred, on one level, to metrical time-counts), the poem answers "yes," building again to the pentameter:

> For I have known them all already, known them all:—
> Have known the evenings, mornings, afternoons,
> I have measured out my life with coffee-spoons;
> I know the voices dying with a dying fall
> Beneath the music from a farther room.
>   So how should I presume?

The previous pentameter stanza, the fourth, fell into the meter as into sleep and woke at the mention of a question. This time, however, the poem enters the pentameter with a conscious act of self-assurance in an iambic hexameter, the claim that "I have known them all already." Read as an affirmation of continuity with the past (Julia M. Reibetanz notes that the "great [blank verse] practitioners of the past always seemed to sound through Eliot's own attempts at the form" [420]), this line enables the next few pentameters. But almost immediately after those flat, resigned lines occurs the next metrical-code twist; the voices that provide the continuity are "dying." The embedded pentameter—"the voices dying with a dying fall"—brings out the difficulty of "presuming" to write in a dead meter, and the question this time is no longer implied but explicit.

The fear of presumption is strong enough to lead to a long interlude almost entirely in free verse, which brings the poem once again to the point of pentameter with the line "And in short, I was afraid." This fear is the strongest motive yet for adopting the pentameter, and the following stanza will be the last one in which the meter is approached and abandoned. It constitutes one of a pair of symmetrical stanzas, one primarily pentameter and one in free verse, each beginning with "and would it have been worth it after all" and ending with the cutting remark, "that is not what I meant at all." These two stanzas bring the whole metrical question to its head. The first, responding to the fear brought out by the preceding free-verse interlude, tries out the possibility of pentameter and approaches the "overwhelming question" more directly than any other point in the poem:

> Would it have been worth while,
> To have bitten off the matter with a smile,
> To have squeezed the universe into a ball
> To roll it towards some overwhelming question,
> To say: "I am Lazarus, come from the dead,
> Come back to tell you all, I shall tell you all"—
> If one, settling a pillow by her head,
>   Should say: "That is not what I meant at all.
>   That is not it, at all."

The passage confronts all the major drawbacks and impediments to iambic pentameter in the poem. The phrases "bitten off the matter with a smile" and "squeezed the universe into a ball" point to the limitations of iambic pentameter as the modernists perceived them: false simplicity and reductionism. The "overwhelming" metrical question mentioned at the beginning of the poem is evoked again. The figure of Lazarus, confirming that death can become life and a dead meter a living one, resolves the previous association of the meter with dead voices. The two triple substitutions in the Lazarus line also point ahead to the redeeming value of the dactylic rhythm in Eliot's later poetry.

In spite of the boldness with which the poem approaches the pentameter here, however, the meter is rejected: "that is not what I meant at all." The poem, immediately responding to the lack of approval for the pentameter in this passage, tries the opposite tack, a passage of identical length in free verse, opening with the identical line, "And would it have been worth it, after all." But the free verse is no more successful than the pentameter, and this response is the same: "that is not what I meant, at all."

Having experimented with both metrical alternatives in such a controlled fashion, "Prufrock" is finally able to make a metrical choice.[17] The rest of the poem is virtually solid iambic pentameter after the one hexameter line, "No, I am not Prince Hamlet, nor was meant to be." The rejection of Hamlet-like indecisiveness in this line propels a pentameter passage so regular and "over-finished" that Pound tried to persuade Eliot to omit it (Kenner 37). The passage is defiant in its affirmation of pentameter while acknowledging all its embarrassing limitations in the age of modernism:

> Deferential, glad to be of use,
> Politic, cautious, and meticulous;
> Full of high sentence, but a bit obtuse;
> At times, indeed, almost ridiculous . . .

A few irregular lines follow, including an echo of the previous "do I dare" dilemma—now a more lighthearted sounding question, since the dilemma has been resolved: "Do I dare to eat a peach?" Then "Prufrock" concludes with a long passage of iambic pentameter. These short stanzas, each entirely pentameter, reiterate the drowning imagery that characterized the only previous entire pentameter stanza in the poem: "I should have been a pair of ragged claws / Scuttling across the floors of silent seas." But now, after the overwhelming question has been more directly faced, the drowning is perhaps a little more pleasant, softened by the company of pentameter "sea-girls" and accompanied by "human voices" instead of the nonhuman, disembodied claws. It is drowning nonetheless. The same "lingering" that led to an iambic pentameter sleep near the opening of "Prufrock" has finally brought the poem to drown in the canonical meter, a drowning that silences the poem and brings it to an end:

> We have lingered in the chambers of the sea
> By sea-girls wreathed with seaweed red and brown
> Till human voices wake us, and we drown.

The Waste Land

In terms of the metrical code, *The Waste Land* begins where
"Prufrock" leaves off. "Prufrock" confronts fears of the shallowness
and deadness of iambic pentameter before eventually giving in to the
traditional meter. *The Waste Land,* taking the possibility of the pen-
tameter initially as a given, engages the problems of the pentameter
on a deeper level and picks up the metrical alternative that had been
developed in the nineteenth century, the triple foot. The dactyls in
The Waste Land are a sign of a reemergence of interest in the triple
foot as the controversy over vers libre waned. They presage the more
direct and widespread Whitmanic influence that characterized the sec-
ond wave of free verse later in the century.

"Prufrock" brought in the pentameter with its second line. *The
Waste Land,* which has less need to grapple with the pentameter be-
cause "Prufrock" has already done so, maintains its initial free-verse
accentual rhythm for over fifty lines. The only exception occurs at
lines 19 through 21, the first three lines quoted:

> What are the roots that clutch, what branches grow
> Out of this stony rubbish? Son of man,
> You cannot say, or guess, for you know only
> A heap of broken images, where the sun beats,
> And the dead tree gives no shelter.

This brief evocation of the pentameter, with its growth imagery,
stands out as a possible moment of hope in the confusion of the
poem's opening images. But the person addressed is incapable of
comprehending such hope, and the pentameter is quickly rejected as
the poem moves back to irregular verse through a rough five-stress
line: "A heap of broken images, where the sun beats." By the time
the poem moves into its first extended pentameter passage at the close
of section 1, the hope the pentameter offered has been transformed
into despair. The faceless crowd in the "Unreal City" shuffles along
in dull, mechanical pentameters with almost no rhythmical variation
or enjambment:

> And each man fixed his eyes before his feet.
> Flowed up the hill and down King William Street,
> To where Saint Mary Woolnoth kept the hours
> With a dead sound on the final stroke of nine.

Winifred Crombie has noted that Eliot's use of the the word "feet" tends to seem self-referential; in the line, "and each man fixed his eyes before his feet," the hypnotic monotony of the pentameters appears to have become so extreme that even the poem itself is aware of it (15).

But the dead meter, like the corpse planted by the speaker's acquaintance, Stetson, in his garden, is still capable of sprouting. Beginning with the very next section, which opens with the Shakespeare-inspired line "the Chair she sat in, like a burnished throne," the pentameter takes on more complex associations.[18] The pentameter rhythm is undisturbed in the vision of the woman at her dressing table, until her perfumes confuse the senses:

> In vials of ivory and coloured glass
> Unstoppered, lurked her strange synthetic perfumes,
> Unguent, powdered, or liquid—troubled, confused
> And drowned the sense in odours; stirred by the air . . .

This sensually induced confusion among the more regular pentameters foreshadows the scenes of betrayal, often sexual betrayal, that most of the rest of the pentameters in the poem describe, and which later in *The Waste Land* spur the adoption of a dactylic alternative. The first such scene occurs in the description of the painting of Philomel, a woman whose brother-in-law raped her and cut out her tongue, but who wove a tapestry to tell the story and eventually escaped as a nightingale:

> Above the antique mantel was displayed
> As though a window gave upon the sylvan scene
> The change of Philomel, by the barbarous king
> So rudely forced; yet there the nightingale
> Filled all the desert with inviolable voice
> And still she cried, and still the world pursues,
> "Jug Jug" to dirty ears.
> And other withered stumps of time . . .

Eliot cites book 4 of *Paradise Lost* for the phrase "sylvan scene"; Milton uses those words to describe Eden as Satan enters it for the first time. Metrically, the single hexameter that separates the pentameter description of the dressing room from the pentameter description of the rape acts as a frame or window, introducing the image of violation into the pentameters as the line introduces Satan into Eden. After the brief description of the rape, however, the poem shifts abruptly out of the pentameter as soon as Philomel-turned-nightingale speaks in her own, no-longer-human voice: "'Jug Jug' to dirty ears." The pentameter has participated in a violation, and the abused victim is now capable only of irregular verse—which is, perhaps, a more "inviolable voice."

Two further, subtler betrayals occupy the pentameters that occur between this scene of sexual betrayal and the next. The woman at the dressing table violates the meter in her turn, taking a kind of revenge for the story of Philomela in the preceding pentameters by transforming the meter which has described her so lushly into a flat and nagging rhythm with her own speech: "I never know what you are thinking. Think." The next pentameters in the poem, at the opening of section 3, "The Fire Sermon," show a similar abrupt shift from the lyrical to the oppressively mundane. The same meter that addresses the Spenser-inspired invocation to the river, "Sweet Thames run softly till I end my song," turns into the image of a rat, "dragging its slimy belly on the bank."[19] Followed by another echo of the Philomela story, the lines "Jug jug jug jug jug jug / So rudely forc'd / Tereu," the pentameter introduces its second scene of sexual betrayal, in which the patronizing clerk makes love to the indifferent typist. A less dramatic scene than the rape of Philomela but just as alienating, this episode shows the two modern lovers participating more or less equally in their dehumanizing encounter. This betrayal of sexuality and of the spirit essentially ends the pentameters in the poem, although before the meter disappears, a line from *The Tempest* and a few lines in praise of London admit one final possibility of its validity. After the next section, "Death by Water," which evokes the drowning at the end of "Prufrock," a new metrical idiom begins.

The last section of *The Waste Land,* "What the Thunder Said," is the most complex on the metrical-code level. The general movement is from pentameters to dactyls. The dactylic movement in the last section is pervasive, unanticipated within the poem, and forms a dramatic contrast to the pentameters and free verse of the preceding sections. The poem begins with several pentameters that evoke, in the allusions to the betrayal of Jesus, the other betrayals that the pentameter has described throughout the poem:

After the torchlight red on sweaty faces
After the frosty silence in the gardens
After the agony in stony places
. . . .
He who was living is now dead
We who were living are now dying.

The pentameter that describes the betrayal shifts to a dactylic move-
ment in the last two lines quoted above, as the death is accepted as a
spiritual opportunity. But the poem continues to shift between the
two meters:

Rock and no water and the sandy road
The road winding above among the mountains
Which are mountains of rock without water
If there were water we should stop and drink
Amongst the rock one cannot stop or think
Sweat is dry and feet are in the sand.

While the dactylic line in this passage is an objective description
("mountains of rock without water"), the pentameter lines complain
about the lack of water. The monotonous regularity of these pen-
tameters, the last extended pentameter passage in the poem, recalls
the description of the crowd in the "Unreal City" in section 1. The
passage on dryness eventually dwindles into an interlude of short
lines, a kind of gasping for water:

If there were water
And no rock
If there were rock
And also water
And water
A spring
. . . . .
But there is no water

Who is the third who walks always beside you?
. . . .
There is always another one walking beside you
Gliding wrapt in a brown mantle, hooded
I do not know whether a man or a woman.

The final gasp for water is answered by the introduction of the myste-
rious "third" whose entrance, in the second line quoted above, intro-
duces the first consistent dactylic rhythm in the entire poem. Samuel
Musgrove traces the origin of this gliding figure to the "dark mother"
in Whitman's "When Lilacs Last in the Dooryard Bloomed" and
notes that the following three stanzas contain further echoes of
Whitman's poem:

> The poetical details which cluster around this central core of
> emotion [the hooded figure] are so numerous that the lines which
> follow in *The Waste Land* can be set out one by one with the
> corresponding phrases from Whitman alongside. Most of these
> occur in the second half of stanza 14 [in "Lilacs"], but one or two
> are from the two stanzas following. They constitute their own
> commentary. (76)

In view of Musgrove's observation about the two poems' wording
and imagery, the dactylic rhythm of this passage, introduced here for
the first time in *The Waste Land,* also reflects Whitman's influence.[20]
The mysterious figure could be either "a man or a woman," main-
taining the nineteenth-century association of dactyls with feminiza-
tion, as do the lines at the beginning of the following stanza: "What
is that sound high in the air / Murmur of maternal lamentation."
Perhaps the most significant aspect of the dactylic rhythm at this
point in the poem, however (and the aspect that will have the most
bearing on the poem's ending) is that its introduction ends the ago-
nized awareness of drought that begins this section. Occurring so
directly after the complaints that there is no water, the third person
and the triple meter arrive as a kind of nourishing rain, an association
that the rest of the poem reinforces.

The remaining pentameters in the poem lay to rest any objections
to abandoning the meter in favor of dactyls. The lines "a woman
drew her long black hair out tight / And fiddled whisper music on
those strings," lines taken from an earlier poem of Eliot's (Aiken
196), indulge in a brief nostalgic sadness, emphasized by the descrip-
tion of the "tower / tolling reminiscent bells." But the following line,
containing an embedded pentameter, clearly reveals the emptiness of
the pentameter "voice" and its inability to provide water for the
drought: "And voices singing out of empty cisterns and exhausted

wells." One more pentameter moves the meter's connotations even further towards desolation, though maintaining a hint of traditional sanctity: "Over the tumbled graves, about the chapel." The image of the chapel continues in irregular verse:

> Over the tumbled graves, about the chapel.
> There is the empty chapel, only the wind's home.
> It has no windows, and the door swings,
> Dry bones can harm no one.
> Only a cock stood on the rooftree
> Co co rico co co rico
> In a flash of lightning. Then a damp gust
> Bringing rain . . .

On a metrical-code level, the image of the chapel embodies the traditional literary sanctity of the pentameter, and this passage demonstrates the archaic and hollow nature of that sanctity. The subsequent assertion that "dry bones can harm no one" indicates that the meter can be abandoned with impunity, while the image of the cock crowing, which echoes the allusions to Gethsemane at the beginning of this section, reiterates the continual imagery of betrayal throughout the poem and offers a final justification for abandoning the meter.

As if the final inhibitions about instituting a metrical alternative have been laid to rest with this imagery, the rain foreshadowed at the first introduction of the dactyls in the mysterious "third" passage now begins. A few lines later, a dactylic or triple rhythm enters the poem as the thunder says *datta,* a Sanskrit word meaning "give":

> what have we given?
> . . . .
> The awful daring of a moment's surrender
> Which an age of prudence can never retract
> By this, and this only, we have existed.

Like the feminized associations of the dactyls earlier in this section, the idea of a sublime "surrender" echoes dactylic connotations in the nineteenth-century poets discussed earlier. It brings to mind a phrase like Whitman's "to launch off with absolute faith" ("Song of the Answerer") or even Crane's "I knew not the ways of my feet" (poem 20). Eliot's dactylic lines here tend to be much less obviously so than those of his predecessors, particularly Whitman. Except for the line beginning "by this, and this only," each of the dactylic lines in the passage above begins with two rising feet, which disguises the falling triple rhythm to some extent. This metrical hesitancy parallels the fear and inhibition expressed in the words of the passage.

After the second word of the thunder, *dayadhvam* [sympathize], the dactylic rhythm continues more subtly than before, and the imagery shifts to that of imprisonment: "I have heard the key / Turn in the door once and turn once only / We think of the key, each in his prison." The prison imagery confirms the fear of having indulged in irrevocable "awful daring," expressed in the preceding dactylic passage.

Eliot's "expressed aversion to Whitman's form and content," which has been documented by Musgrove (15), no doubt contributed to the ambivalence towards the dactylic rhythm evident in the *datta* and *dayadhvam* passages. The passages associate the dactylic rhythm with rain, a healing answer to the debilitating drought. But in each case the healing is brief—"a moment's surrender," "[re]vive for a moment." Each small redemption also involves regret and a sense of limitation. In view of Whitman's use of dactylic rhythms, the sense of frustrated imprisonment evident in the *dayadhvam* passage reflects Eliot's image, in a 1919 review, of Whitman (and Poe) as "bulbs in a glass bottle," which "could only exhaust what was in them" (qtd. in Musgrove 35).

The use of dactylic rhythms in the *datta* and *dayadhvam* passages maintains nineteenth-century dactylic connotations, associating the dactyls with traditionally feminized, emotional kinds of activities— giving and sympathizing. A feminized meter is not, presumably, as appropriate in response to the last of the thunder's words, *damyata* [control]. The meter appears only briefly in the short passage which follows the word *damyata*. The passage juxtaposes a rough pentameter with one line ending in a dactylic rhythm and one line of free verse: "the sea was calm, your heart would have responded / Gaily, when invited, beating obedient / To controlling hands." The dactylic rhythm here occurs only in the middle line; though it has the integrity of a heartbeat, it remains "invited" and "obedient," contained by the pentameter and the free verse that surround it. Having been thus harnessed and controlled, the dactylic power disappears from the poem.

The last stanza of *The Waste Land* returns to some of the same problems with the pentameter confronted earlier. The stanza begins in trochaic meters, and iambic pentameter occurs in only two disturbing lines, the last lines in English in the poem:

> I sat upon the shore
> Fishing, with the arid plain behind me
> Shall I at least set my lands in order?
> London Bridge is falling down falling down falling down
> *Poi s'ascose nel foco che gli affina*
> *Quando fiam utt chelidon*—O swallow swallow
> *Le Prince d'Aquitaine a la tour abolie*
> These fragments I have shored against my ruins
> Why then Ile fit you. Hieronymo's mad againe.
> Datta. Dayadhvam. Damyata.
> Shantih shantih shantih

The rest of the stanza, however, brings back imagery associated with the pentameter throughout the poem and moves the stanza towards the final pentameters. The fishing king is facing water—perhaps the water mentioned most recently in the poem, the rain and "Ganga" (the river Ganges). Water has been associated with dactyls and land with iambic pentameter throughout the poem. As he thinks of setting "lands in order," the king turns his attention away from the dactylic rhythm and towards the "arid plain," echoing the desert landscape described in the pentameters at the beginning of the section.

The poem having focused again on the pentameter through the land imagery, its next lines are an agonized expression of fear and need of the meter. The collapse of European culture, and English in particular—"London Bridge is falling down"—is not enough to forestall the passionate need for tradition traceable in the allusions to the three poets in the Italian, Latin, and French lines that follow. In the quotation from Dante, one poet dives into a fire that is refining his soul, a fire as painful and necessary as a confrontation with the aridity of the pentameter. The next poet, in the anonymous Latin poem, dreams of being like the swallow, which brings back the figure of Philomela—in the metrical-code context of this poem, a voice free of the pentameter, but only as a result of having been brutally violated and betrayed by it. The line from the Gerard de Nerval sonnet, spoken by a poet who thinks of himself as a disinherited prince, heir to the French troubadours' tradition, comes closest to a direct nostalgia for the pentameter; the image of the ruined tower resonates with the image of the "empty chapel" that occurs in a pentameter earlier in this section.

Whether or not these three poets have indicated a desire for the pentameter, the line "these fragments I have shored against my ruins" is a clear expression of hope in the persistent power of the pentameter to order poetic experience. The pentameter has witnessed or participated in violation and betrayal during the course of the poem. As a consequence, it has been rejected, missed, and rejected again. In spite of this rejection, and regardless of the preliminary development of an alternative, dactylic, rhythm, this pentameter hangs on as an expression of hope. It is a broken version of the hope evident in the first pentameter in the poem, "what are the roots that clutch, what branches grow." The organic imagery of naturally growing roots and branches has turned into the vision of dead fragments which must be manipulated, "shored," by the poet in order to have any chance of helping him. The poem itself has helped to maim and break the pentameter, and yet the speaker still hopes to gain some salvation from the meter. The last, pentameter line brings in Heironymo from Thomas Kyd's *The Spanish Tragedy,* who feigned madness and wrote a fragmented, crazy play with a real purpose: to avenge his son's murder. The fragmentation in *The Waste Land* is also, metrically, not as complete as it looks, and the devastated pentameter returns at the close of the poem.

Four Quartets

In terms of meter, the task of the *Four Quartets* is to complete the task begun by *The Waste Land* almost twenty years earlier, finally establishing the dactylic rhythm as an alternative to pentameter, as well as to face and transcend the violent emotions inspired by the pentameter in *The Waste Land.* The *Four Quartets* as a whole show a greater equilibrium between the meters throughout than do either of the earlier poems. Pentameters in the *Four Quartets* are much less dominant than in "Prufrock" and less threatening than in *The Waste Land,* while the dactyls are more established and consistent in their appearance than in either "Prufrock" or *The Waste Land.* During the course of the *Four Quartets,* the strong emotions associated with the meters die down, quieting the ambivalence that arose in the wake of the free verse movement.

While dactyls hardly appeared at all in "Prufrock" and only in the last section of *The Waste Land,* they are conspicuous at the very beginning of *Four Quartets.* The opening of "Burnt Norton," in the loose accentual meter that forms the basic metric of the poem as a whole, has a clear dactylic rhythm in the second and third lines: "Time present and time past / Are both perhaps present in time future, / And time future contained in time past." The association of dactyls with time will continue throughout the poem, although, as the only other, and the most emphatic, dactylic line in the poem's opening emphasizes, it is often a special, timeless time: "Point to one end, which is always present." The poem continues in accentual meter throughout the long passage leading up to the sudden spiritual illumination, the vision of the pool filled with water:

> To look down into the drained pool.
> Dry the pool, dry concrete, brown edged,
> And the pool was filled with water out of sunlight,
> And the lotos rose, quietly, quietly,
> The surface glittered out of heart of light,
> And they were behind us, reflected in the pool.

The four-stress accentual meter, still present in the first two lines quoted, gives way suddenly to the first pentameter in the poem at the moment that the pool fills with water. This pentameter is followed by a dactylic line, a completely regular pentameter line, and another pentameter.

The pentameter and dactylic rhythms each contribute to the fullness of the vision described in this passage; metrically, the transcendent peace of the vision is the result of their harmonious interaction. The dactylic line (also scannable as anapests)[21] describes both the development of the vision and its nature deep within the water: "And the lotos rose, quietly, quietly." The completely regular pentameter, by contrast, describes the water's surface at one particular instant: "The surface glittered out of heart of light." The duple and triple meters, and the two perspectives on the experience, blend in the two pentameters that sandwich these two key lines. The first, "and the pool was filled with water out of sunlight," is a pentameter (with an initial triple substitution and a falling rhythm in the feminine ending) that describes not only the pool filling with water, a development over time like the rising of the lotus, but the sunlight on the water. The other pentameter, "and they were behind us, reflected in the pool," has two triple substitutions, in the second and third feet. It combines a description of the pool's reflective surface with a consciousness of the three-dimensional, reflected reality.

At the height of this transcendental vision, the pentameters' emphasis on surfaces is an essential part of the experience. By the time the vision is over, however, the emphasis on surfaces has become a restriction. Two lines after the vision disappears, the final pentameter in this part of the poem confirms the limitations of human perception: "Go, go, go, said the bird: human kind / Cannot bear very much reality." After several long stanzas of philosophical meditation in accentual and prose rhythms, a few pentameters recur in the description of people on a train in section 3. Each of these also describes shallowness, a rejection of deeper realities: "Distracted from distraction by distraction"; "Not here the darkness, in this twittering world." Even when a few further pentameters appear in the call to "descend lower," they indicate a lack of internal as well as external resources:

> Internal darkness, deprivation
> And destitution of all property,
> Dessication of the world of sense,
> Evacuation of the world of fancy,
> Inoperancy of the world of spirit . . .

In contrast to the opening dactylic evocation of a timeless present, repeated at the end of the vision of the pool—"Point to one end, which is always present," the final pentameter in section 3 concentrates on the past and the future only; it describes the world moving "in appetancy, on its metalled ways / of time past and time future."

Throughout the rest of "Burnt Norton," the same opposition persists. Dactyls participate in possibilities of spiritual fulfillment: "Will the sunflower turn to us, will the clematis / Stray down, bend to us; tendril and spray"; "Words, after speech, reach / Into the silence"; "Love is itself unmoving, / Only the cause and end of movement, / Timeless, and undesiring." The pentameter reappears only once, juxtaposing two previous connotations of spiritual deadness in a description of how the Word in the desert "Is most attacked by voices of temptation, / the crying shadow in the funeral dance." The idea of temptation evokes the spiritual weakness developed in conjunction with the pentameter in "Burnt Norton"; the funeral dance brings back the desolation and deadness of the graveyard and ruined chapel in the pentameters at the end of *The Waste Land*.

Although the dactylic connotations at the end of "Burnt Norton" include the only images of redemption in the poem so far, they also revive the ambivalence towards dactyls at the end of *The Waste Land*—the sense that dactylic surrender would be an "awful daring." The people on the subway are plagued by dactyls, "filled with fancies and empty of meaning," as well as by the pentameter, "distracted from distraction by distraction." The "Word in the desert" may be "most attacked" by the temptation of the facile and empty pentameter, but it is also suffers from the expressive inadequacy of the dactyl:

Words strain,
Crack and sometimes break, under the burden,
Under the tension . . .
. . . .
shrieking voices
Scolding, mocking, or merely chattering
Always assail them.

For all its redemptive promise, the dactylic rhythm threatens Eliot for some of the same reasons that it bothered Whitman and Crane; ultimately it represents a force basically opposed to "meaning," to language, and to the rational thought on which his poems so often rely. The "shrieking" voices here also reinforce his association, like that of his predecessors, between dactylic irrationality and the feminine.

"East Coker" continues the process of establishing the dactylic rhythm as a workable alternative to the pentameter. The opening of the poem includes a single pentameter line that refers to the meter as an old structure, but one that can be "restored":

In my beginning is my end. In succession
Houses rise and fall, crumble, are extended,
Are removed, destroyed, restored, or in their place
Is an open field, or a factory, or a by-pass.

The description of the country dance in the next stanza accomplishes the restoration:

> In that open field
> If you do not come too close, if you do not come too close,
> On a summer midnight, you can hear the music
> Of the weak pipe and the little drum
> And see them dancing around the bonfire
> The association of man and woman
> In daunsinge, signifying matrimonie.

The initial pentameter in this section, "on a summer midnight, you can hear the music," is quite regular and firmly establishes the "music" that can be traced in the subsequent pentameters. The "restored" pentameter now inhabits the "open field" described at the poem's opening, but the availability of the meter is qualified, like that of the dance: "if you do not come too close."

The poem keeps the remaining pentameters in the passage at a distance, either with archaic language, as in the last line quoted above, or with the defamiliarizing omission of the first syllable, as in the last pentameter in the section: "lifting heavy feet in clumsy shoes." Like the line "and each man fixed his eyes before his feet" in *The Waste Land,* this line calls attention to the shortcomings of its own meter with the punning use of the word "feet." The word recurs in the next line, "earth feet, loam feet," and then, as if the archaic meter had spurred the thought of death, the dancers are suddenly "long since under the earth" in the following line. Reinforcing the clumsy dead pentameter with a new kind of "music," a pronounced dactylic rhythm enters the poem here, briefly, for the first time: "Keeping time, / Keeping the rhythm in their dancing." But the pentameter's distance from the scene allows it to close the section with a general meditation on "the time of the seasons and the constellations / The time of milking and the time of harvest," which ends this section.

Section 2 evokes both meters only briefly in order to acknowledge each of their limitations. The lines,

> There is, it seems to us,
> At best, only a limited value
> In the knowledge derived from experience.
> The knowledge imposes a pattern, and falsifies

question the value of the dactylic rhythm for the first time. The dactylic connotations here are those of immediate experience as opposed to inherited or traditional knowledge, connotations also evident in Whitman. A final key line in section 2, about the "folly" of old men, expresses fear of both meters at once: "their fear of fear and frenzy, their fear of possession." After the first two words, the line contains an embedded pentameter (with a trochee in the fourth foot and a feminine ending). Simultaneously, beginning with the word "frenzy," it consists of two pronounced dactyls and a trochee. Associating the pentameter with a threatening tradition and the dactyl with loss of control, the line initiates the former meter with the concept of fear and the latter with frenzy; but the fear of possession by each is equally strong.

In section 3, these limitations and fears are transformed into more transcendental renunciations as Eliot associates each meter with the idea of non-attachment. Both meters appear briefly amid the lines in accentual and prose rhythms that develop the mystical idea of spiritual redemption through disownment. In the case of the dactyl the nonattachment involves emotions:

> wait without hope
> For hope would be hope for the wrong thing; wait without love
> For love would be love of the wrong thing; there is yet faith
> But the faith and the love and the hope are all in the waiting.

In the case of the pentameter, the nonattachment involves ownership: "and what you own is what you do not own." The line is consistent with a similar pentameter statement in "Burnt Norton": "and destitution of all property." Here, however, the nonattachment is phrased in positive rather than in negative terms.

If, at this stage, both meters are on somewhat equal "foot"ing—the fear of each having been acknowledged, and each having been associated with some kind of redemption through renunciation—section 4 more fully develops each of their distinctive qualities. Here each meter conveys the spiritual attitude that it might have embodied in the nineteenth century: the pentameter, conventional religion, and the dactyl, mystical, intuitive spirituality. The pentameter, but not the dactyl, appears among the explicitly Judeo-Christian imagery and insistent tetrameters early in section 4: "But to remind of our, and

Adam's curse"; "That we are sound, substantial flesh and blood."
After these lines the meter is abandoned. Reconciliation is achieved
in the last section of the poem, as at the end of "Burnt Norton," with
dactylic rhythms: "For us, there is only the trying."

> Love is most nearly itself
> When here and now cease to matter . . .
> We must be still and still moving
> Into another intensity
> For a further union, a deeper communion.

The only pentameter in this passage is a negative one and describes a
hindrance to be overcome by the dactyls: "Through the dark cold and
the empty desolation." The development of each meter's spiritual
quality at the end of "East Coker" marks a turning point. The rest
of the *Four Quartets* moves, however haltingly, towards a reconcili-
ation with both meters.

Metrically, "The Dry Salvages" is a climactic poem in the *Four
Quartets*. After all the ambivalence towards both pentameters and
dactyls in the two preceding poems, "The Dry Salvages,"well-
recognized as the most Whitmanian of the quartets, finally accepts
the dactyl. The dactylic rhythms that resolved tension and expressed
spiritual closure at the end of both "Burnt Norton" and "East Coker"
blossom into a more pervasive presence. "The Dry Salvages" intro-
duces the meter as a regular metrical option, a movement which
allows the pentameter to return in a less overwhelming manner. Since
the pentameter is no longer the only metrical alternative to irregular
verse, it can be adopted without threatening to dominate the poem.

"The Dry Salvages" opens with a highly conspicuous dactylic
rhythm: "I do not know much about gods; but I think that the river
/ Is a strong brown god—sullen, untamed and intractable." Lasting
throughout the whole long first stanza, this dactylic rhythm is main-
tained longer within lines, and lasts for more lines, than any other in
the *Four Quartets*. Helen Gardner even refers to the meter of this passage
as accentual hexameter, "the rhythm of 'Evangeline'" (34). The sense
of this passage, a description of the development of a river from an
"untrustworthy" "frontier" to a "problem confronting the builder of
bridges," until finally it is conquered and "almost forgotten," is the
story of development of the attitude towards dactylic rhythms in the

poem up to this point—the point when, its wildness forgotten, it is being used as the fundamental metric of an opening passage.

The image of the tamed river leads, however, to a reminder that the river is still "keeping his seasons and rages, destroyer, reminder / Of what men choose to forget." This idea sets up the potential need for a countermeter that is more oriented towards human experience. The two following very regular pentameters, the only ones in this section, introduce the first mention of human artifacts into the catalog of natural phenomena that opens the second stanza: "it tosses up our losses, the torn seine, / The shattered lobsterpot, the broken oar." The strength of the dactylic opening frees the poem to express a nostalgia, through the pentameter images of the net, the oar, and the lobsterpot, for the human skills and traditions that the pentameter connotes. Except perhaps for the Christian imagery in section 4 of "East Coker," these are the two most potentially positive pentameters in all of *Four Quartets* up to this point. As if to emphasize that both meters are beginning to coexist for the first time, these pentameters are followed by the statement that "the sea has many voices, / Many gods and many voices."

But the harmony of coexisting meters and voices pulls apart, as it has so many other times in *Four Quartets*. The poem continues with a description of the sea as a wild, nonhuman place, whose voices include the "sea howl," the "sea yelp," and the "whine in the rigging." The alien quality is made explicit, and equated with a dactylic rhythm, in the statement,

> the tolling bell
> Measures time not our time, rung by the unhurried
> Ground swell, a time
> Older than the time of chronometers.

This brief passage reiterates the dactylic otherness evident in the lines about the river that is a "destroyer, reminder / Of what men choose to forget."

At the same time that the dactylic rhythm grows in wildness, increasingly separated from the previous moment of harmony, the pentameter grows in nostalgia. The two meters cross paths while they are separated, however, and take on some of each others' characteristics. Section 2 opens with a long fixed-rhyme scheme, the only one in the *Quartets,* consisting of six roughly accentual six-line stanzas, each using the same rhyme sounds in the same sequence. Under cover of this extremely tight form, as if the exact rhyme scheme is meant to distract the reader's attention from the changing metrical connotations, the shift takes place. The rhymed poem begins with impatience about pentameter nostalgia: "where is there an end of it, the soundless wailing, / The silent withering of autumn flowers." The next pentameters in the poem repeat the same theme:

> There is no end of it, the voiceless wailing
> No end to the withering of withered flowers,
> To the movement of pain that is painless and motionless,
> To the drift of the sea and the drifting wreckage.

The pentameters here take on a slight triple rhythm as well as some of the dactylic qualities of the third, dactylic line that interrupts them; they are voiceless, involve paradoxical "painless pain," and are associated with the sea. At the same time, the dactylic rhythm takes on a new twist; the only extended dactylic passage in this section states,

> We cannot think of a time that is oceanless
> Or of an ocean not littered with wastage
> Or of a future that is not liable
> Like the past, to have no destination.

The metrical-code meaning is that any time, any meter, is an ocean like the dactyl—but that any ocean carries human wastage as does the pentameter. The dactylic ocean is inextricably twined with the pentameter, and even if there is a dactylic future, it will end up with no destination, like the pentameter past. The acceptance of this vision enables the realization, near the end of section 2, that "time the destroyer is time the preserver." The dactylic threat is defused, and the dactyl becomes reliable as it was not earlier. The image of "the ragged rock in the restless water" that closes the section's final meditation is a reassuring one; no matter what the weather, the rock "is what it always was."

The pentameter threat is also neutralized, as the image of people on the train counterbalances the pentameter shallowness in the vision of the train in "Burnt Norton." Here, the pentameter is no longer a

distraction but accepted as a human relief, without its previous con-
notations:

> (And those who saw them off have left the platform)
> Their faces relax from grief into relief,
> To the sleepy rhythm of a hundred hours.
> Fare forward, travellers! not escaping from the past
> Into different lives, or into any future;
> You are not the same people who left that station
> Or who will arrive at any terminus,
> While the narrowing rails slide together behind you;
> And on the deck of the drumming liner
> Watching the furrow that widens behind you,
> You shall not think "the past is finished"
> Or "the future is before us."

The Whitmanic echoes in this passage—among them the exclamation
points, the exhortative mode, and the dactylic image of the furrow
behind the boat as in "Crossing Brooklyn Ferry"—also emphasize
that the dactyl, as well as the pentameter, has been accepted at this
point in the poem.

Metrically, the remainder of the "The Dry Salvages" is remark-
ably symmetrical compared with the endings of "Burnt Norton" and
"East Coker." The poem ends with evocations of transcendence simi-
lar to the endings of the two previous poems, but this time, although
the dactyl still closes the poem, both meters are involved. The figure
embodying this final metrical harmony is the Incarnation:

> The hint half guessed, the gift half understood, is Incarnation.
> Here the impossible union
> Of spheres of existence is actual,
> Here the past and future
> Are conquered, and reconciled.

An embedded pentameter precedes the phrase "is Incarnation," and
several dactylic lines pick up the theme, continuing the explanation
of incarnation; both meters participate equally in the description. This
incarnation is possible because the meters have taken on each others'
characteristics by this point. The last pentameter line in the poem, at
the end of section 4, describes the throat of the sea, an image that

would have been dactylic earlier in the poem: "in the sea's lips / Or in the dark throat which will not reject them." The last line of the poem, on the other hand, uses the meter previously associated with water to describe the soil, no longer the "arid plain" of *The Waste Land* but "the life of significant soil."

By the opening of "Little Gidding," both meters have been so established that they appear briefly without interrupting the overall accentual rhythm. In contrast to the strongly dactylic opening of "The Dry Salvages," section 1 of "Little Gidding" consists of virtually uninterrupted accentual lines. The dactylic rhythm occurs in the second line, "semipiternal though sodden towards sundown," and the pentameter in the fifth line, "the brief sun flames the ice, on ponds and ditches"; both are incorporated seamlessly into the general movement.

In each quartet, section 2 opens with a conspicuously formal section, a metrical chant. Section 2 of "Little Gidding" clarifies the new role of the dactylic rhythm in this poem. In each of the first two quartets, iambic tetrameter satisfies the demand for formal regularity in the second section, and "The Dry Salvages" uses an elaborate rhyme scheme that modulates between a pentameter-based line and a dactylic rhythm for the same function. Section 2 of "Little Gidding," however, is the first such formal section in *Four Quartets* to use a recurrent dactylic rhythm as its only formal device. Short lines with a dactylic rhythm, such as "Ash on an old man's sleeve," "Dust in the air suspended," and "This is the death of air" replace the iambic tetrameters from section 2 of the first two quartets, demonstrating that the triple rhythm is now a firmly established metrical alternative.

Just as the formal part of section 2 dramatically reconciles the poem with dactyls, the lengthy description of the "familiar compound ghost" later in section 2 reconciles the poem with pentameter. The passage is in straight blank verse, a remarkable and conspicuous use of the meter so sporadically used earlier in *Four Quartets*.[22] The ghost speaks as if the pentameter had finally been given a voice to express itself, fully developing the previous glancing references and brief acknowledgments of the fears of the canonical meter. By the time the ghost fades from sight, the pentameter and the dactyl are both accepted metrical idioms.

A "compound ghost," a "dead master . . . both one and many," is a perfect figure for a meter that bears the weight of many previous poets in its single rhythmic pattern:

> I caught the sudden look of some dead master
> Whom I had known, forgotten, half recalled
>> Both one and many; in the brown baked features
>> The eyes of a familiar compound ghost
> Both intimate and unidentifiable.

The pentameter soon demonstrates some of the negative connotations it carries elsewhere in Eliot. The narrator describes his walk with the ghost as they speak: "we trod the pavement in a dead patrol." The word "trod" in this context echoes the images of dead and clumsy feet in *The Waste Land* and "East Coker." But the ghost chooses not to recount most of the problems of the meter at this point, reminding the narrator-poet that his own practice will cause its own new burdens for subsequent poets:

> And he: I am not eager to rehearse
>> My thoughts and theory which you have forgotten.
>> These things have served their purpose: let them be.
> So with your own, and pray they be forgiven
>> By others, as I pray you to forgive.

Surprising even himself with the words he is speaking, the ghost emphasizes that the old meter can coexist with new diction. In view of Steele's point that the revolt against meter was intimately connected with a rejection of Victorian poetic idiom, the metrical-code message is that the connection is no longer necessary:

>> For last year's words belong to last year's language
>> And next year's words await another voice.
>> . . . .
> So I find words I never thought to speak
>> In streets I never thought I should revisit.

After these reassurances, however, the ghost also recapitulates some of the major problems of the pentameter, inspiring the narrator ultimately to break out of the strict meter and back to a looser iambic-based line by the end of the passage. The first problem is the emptiness of an inherited, and possibly worn and inappropriate, poetic idiom:

> First, the cold friction of expiring sense
> Without enchantment, offering no promise
> But bitter tastelessness of shadow fruit
> As body and soul begin to fall asunder.

The common free-verse call for organic form, for a poetic body that drew its shape from the individual poem's soul, responds to just such a perception. The ghost's second point conveys helpless frustration with the monumental strength of a now frivolous and meaningless poetic tradition: "Second, the conscious impotence of rage / At human folly, and the laceration / Of laughter at what ceases to amuse." The ghost's third and final point expresses the disappointment of a poet, strongly rooted in tradition, with the failings of traditional poetic methods:

> And last, the rending pain of re-enactment
> Of all that you have done, and been; the shame
> Of motives late revealed, and the awareness
> Of things ill done and done to others' harm
> Which once you took for exercise of virtue.

With the image of "that refining fire / Where you must move in measure," however, the ghost offers a way out of the dilemma as well as some metrical freedom. The poet is "restored" by leaving the pentameters for a line of hexameter. The return to pentameter occurs in a line more rhythmically graceful than any in the preceding passage, its rhythm enhanced by the alliterating *m:*

> From wrong to wrong the exasperated spirit
> Proceeds, unless restored by that refining fire
> Where you must move in measure, like a dancer.

The final section of "Little Gidding" opens with the assertion that "What we call the beginning is often the end / And to make an end is to make a beginning. / The end is where we start from." This section transforms the pentameter from an ending to a new beginning, and the last pentameter passage in *Four Quartets* shows a new sense of harmony with the traditional meter that is epitomized in the phrase, "an easy commerce of the old and the new." The poem's use of the pentameter, brought to a resolution by the encounter with the ghost, starts again on a more practicable basis:

> An easy commerce of the old and the new,
> The common word exact without vulgarity,
> The formal word precise but not pedantic . . .

Acceptance of the pentameter does not displace the other meters in the poem, however. Like the other quartets, "Little Gidding" ends in irregular rhythms but incorporates dactylic rhythms into its conclusion: "When the tongues of flame are in-folded / Into the crowned knot of fire / And the fire and the rose are one."

The final acceptance of the pentameter in "Little Gidding" completes the movement of the rest of *Four Quartets*. Both the pentameter and the dactylic rhythm are now established metrical options; the negative aspects of each have been acknowledged and overcome. The extended use of both meters in "Little Gidding" actualizes the metrical harmony foreshadowed in the vision of the pool at the beginning of "Burnt Norton." The development of the dactylic rhythm has freed the pentameter of its own dominance, and the last passage of iambic pentameter in *Four Quartets* is the most positive and accepting in any of Eliot's major poems. The problem of metrical connotations has been resolved, and Eliot would write no more major verse.

Perhaps because Eliot had more metrical options at his disposal than any nineteenth-century poet, his poems are more complex in terms of the metrical code than those of his predecessors. The prosody of his major poems, however, shows a clear development: the frightened obsession with readopting the pentameter as a basic meter in "Prufrock" moves, through a sense of betrayal, a repeated rejection of the meter, and the beginnings of establishing a dactylic alternative in *The Waste Land,* to the acceptance of both meters in *Four Quartets.* Eliot accomplished this development by making peace with the inherited nineteenth-century associations carried by the pentameter and the dactylic rhythm. While the connotations were too deep-rooted to be overcome completely, through exploring the old associations and trying out new ones, he was able to temper the fear of the pentameter as a useless, dominating chain and of the dactyl as a violent, nonhuman passion, and thus to reclaim both meters for subsequent poets.

T. S. Eliot is often considered one of the pioneers of free verse. Yet by the time Eliot's most notoriously revolutionary poem, *The Waste Land,* appeared in 1922, the prosodic issues that he addressed for his generation no longer involved the breakdown of traditional meter. Instead the poem's prosody was an attempt to establish a new metrical idiom for a generation jaded and disillusioned with free verse, and exhausted by the apparent lack of any viable prosodic alternative to it. Eliot's poems address the metrical vacuum left by the waning of the first free-verse movement, and they span the period up to the beginning of the next. Eliot was the first major American poet for whom regular meters were available solely as an active choice—a force to add to a poem—instead of as a given to react against. In facing the responsibility of this choice and the challenge of the traditional meters with all of their difficult meanings, Eliot carried American poetry over a crucial prosodic bridge.

Chapter 6

Contemporary Free Verse:
A Postscript

Though the prosody of the late twentieth century seems far removed from that of the mid–nineteenth century, today's free-verse poets are struggling with the same kinds of metrical problems as their nineteenth-century predecessors. Pressure on nineteenth-century free-verse poets to write in meter led to the encoding of powerful and often negative emotions within traditional metrical patterns. Contemporary free-verse poets have instead felt pressure to avoid meter, sometimes as directly as in Robert Bly's statement that "we . . . have no choice but to write in free verse" (38). In this context, meter can take on the lure of the forbidden. Like their predecessors, contemporary poets respond prosodically, embedding emotionally powerful, often positive connotations ranging from reassurance to desire within both the iambic pentameter and the triple rhythm.

This quiet yet momentous change in attitudes towards meter probably occurred during the period at midcentury after the free-verse tradition had been widely established. Through the 1930s the central tradition of metrically variable or free-verse poetry still defined itself primarily in opposition to metered poetry, as poets built on Eliot's idea of meter as a constant presence lurking behind the arras of free verse. The poetic line typical of that time was, as Antony Easthope puts it, a "compromise of 'freed verse' in which the iambic norm, constantly departed from is by that token constantly invoked and so never displaced" (333). Even William Carlos Williams felt the effects of this tendency, as is evident in his effort to define his prosodic practice in terms of metrical feet.

For the free-verse generation that followed, however, both prosodic changes—the claiming of free verse and the validation of traditional meters in free verse—were essentially over. During the decades of the midcentury, free verse lost touch with its metrical history, and traditional meters were less significant in free verse than before or since. The traditional metrical patterns in the work of the generation of poets who matured in the late 1940s, 1950s, and early 1960s—poets like Theodore Roethke, John Berryman, Elizabeth Bishop, Robert Lowell, Adrienne Rich, Anne Sexton, and Sylvia Plath—have insignificant or inconsistent meanings compared with those in the free verse of previous eras.

The pattern of metrical-code meanings in Anne Sexton's "Little Girl, My String Bean, My Lovely Woman" provides clues to the reasons traditional meters were a relatively neutral poetic force for poets of Sexton's generation. The attitude towards the iambic pentameter tradition evoked in these lines is casual, almost playful, without the emotional urgency or seriousness characteristic of iambic pentameters in earlier free verse. The third through fifth lines of the poem, including two of its three iambic pentameters, read as follows:

> Oh darling! Born in that sweet birthday suit
> and having known it and owned it for so long,
> now you must watch high noon enter.

For Sexton, as for other mid-century poets, meter was a poetic "birthday suit."[1] The phrase "having known it and owned it for so long" refers aptly to her experience of the iambic pentameter. Sexton and the poets of her generation were schooled thoroughly in traditional prosody and then encouraged and sanctioned to write in free verse. Their ease of access to both meters compared, for instance, with nineteenth century or contemporary poets, may explain why traditional meter carries little emotional weight in Sexton's prosody and that of her peers.

In "Little Girl, My String Bean, My Lovely Woman," the two initial pentameters lead into the heavily stressed free-verse statement, "now you must watch high noon enter," a line whose meaning suggests that free verse was no less familiar, and probably more inevitable, to Sexton than meter. The prosodic and imagistic opposition between the naked body and noon is subdued, the tone of the free

verse suggesting development more than struggle as the poet medi-
tates on her daughter's coming to maturity.

Sexton's poems sometimes invoke traditional metrical power
only to weaken it through various verbal means, a further indication
that meter was accessible enough for her to reject with relative ease.
The final iambic pentameter in "Little Girl," for instance, uses a com-
plex trope to modify the pentameter, as if approaching the meter
from a safe, hypothetical distance. The line—"there would have been
such ripening within"—is a metapentameter. It introduces a poetic
description of a fantastic X-ray-like look into the speaker's womb
that could be performed by "a magical mother"—someone the
speaker in this poem, however, is not. Through her hypothetical
persona, the poet discounts the authority or blame that attaches to the
metapentameter at the same time she claims its power. Sexton's rare
lines in triple rhythm also evoke traditional connotations, but dis-
tance them verbally with a mild, almost dissociated tone. Phrases like
"into the hypnotist's trance," from "Briar Rose," or "the permanent
guests have done nothing new"—a line in "Flee on Your Donkey"
referring to the inmates of a psychiatric hospital—recall the irrational-
ity and loss of control traditionally associated with triple meters, but
their placid tone dulls the power of their metrical echo.

For poets like Theodore Roethke or Allen Ginsberg, whose free
verse tends to conspicuous, incantatory rhythm, the mid-twentieth-
century prosodic context results not in low-key metrical connotations
but in an internal inconsistency among metrical meanings. Ginsberg's
rhythm has much in common with Whitman's, but Ginsberg does
not maintain patterns of metrical meaning as Whitman does. The
first line of Ginsberg's "Howl" establishes traditional metrical conno-
tations in an idealizing iambic pentameter that gives way in midline
to a series of horrified dactyls: "I saw the best minds of my generation
destroyed by madness, starving hysterical naked." The line's pro-
sodic subtext recalls the New Critical conviction that iambic pen-
tameter is the worthiest meter for ratiocination. The line's opening
embedded iambic pentameter evokes the rational metrical ideal of
Pope and Johnson, while its remaining triple feet describe the an-
guished lives and spiritual vulnerability of Ginsberg's generation.
"Howl" contains many other metrical echoes, including a passionate
description, in common hymn meter, of sex in a Turkish bath: "the

blond and naked angel came to pierce them with a sword." It is
tempting to look for metrical-code patterns in these lines; the use of
hymn meter for the latter subject, for instance, is suggestive in view
of Ginsberg's spiritual atttude towards sex. However, none of these
connotations form a pattern, and the meanings of the other iambic-
pentameter and dactylic phrases in Ginsberg's poem are unrelated to
the traditional connotations of its first line.

The efforts of Whitman and Crane to establish a free-verse alter-
native to the norm of iambic pentameter fully achieved their goal in
the mid–twentieth century. Sexton, Ginsberg, and the other poets of
midcentury wrote free verse more or less on its own terms, referring
back to meter much less, and less urgently, than any poets before
them. This shift in emphasis completely altered the prosodic climate
for poets of the late 1970s and 1980s. Between 1974, when Sexton
wrote "Little Girl," and the end of the decade, when a new poetic
generation came to maturity, the effects of the century's second major
wave of free verse found their way into poetry anthologies and text-
books.[2] New Critical standards and terminology were displaced, and
free verse, now several generations deep, was accepted as a system
of prosody more than it ever had been.

Audre Lorde and Charles Wright are two representative poets
of the generation that emerged into this new prosodic climate. On
the surface, their poetics have little in common but the use of free
verse, very roughly defined. Wright's leisurely meditative poetry
uses the blank space of the page for visual prosodic effects, while
Lorde's speech-based, frequently political verse consists of brief,
emotional, often disjointed phrases. The two poets' tone, syntax, and
diction are markedly different, yet they share a common language of
metrical connotations. Both Lorde and Wright associate the same
cluster of meanings with the iambic pentameter and the dactylic
rhythm, meanings consistent with the connotations carried by metri-
cal patterns in the nineteenth and early twentieth century.

Lorde's and Wright's iambic pentameter and dactylic rhythms
carry more uniformly positive connotations than these meters did for
earlier generations. Lorde, developing out of Dickinson's prosodic
tradition, is less ambivalent about the iambic pentameter and more
likely to use the dactylic rhythm than Dickinson. Wright, following
on Whitman's prosodic legacy, retains none of his predecessor's fre-
quent dislike of the iambic pentameter. Both poets use traditional

metrical associations to carry emotional and spiritual weight at crucial points in their poems.

Wright's sense of the connotations of both iambic pentameter and triple rhythm are strikingly congruous with those of the nineteenth century. A concise couplet near the beginning of his "Journal of English Days" could serve as a mnemonic for the traditional connotations of both meters: "The difference between the spirit and the flesh / is finite, and slowly transgressable." The pentameter, in keeping with metrical-code tradition, refers to apparently objective, socially sanctioned positivist truth—in this case a duality between the physical and spiritual worlds. The second line's three dactyls embody a contrasting view, congruent with traditional dactylic connotations: the belief in overcoming duality through a nonrational holism.[3]

While Wright's dactyls participate in the same complex of meanings as Whitman's, they show a decided shift in emotional tone. At the lyrical climax of Wright's "The Southern Cross," for example, the poet meditates on his sense of exclusion from nature. Repeated dactylic rhythms evoke the world's inhuman, random shifting, as in the lines, "All that we look on is windfall. / All we remember is wind." Like Whitman's "Quicksand Years," Wright's poem ends with a pentameter response to such dactylic shapelessness. Wright's speaker hides from the chaotic wind in an imaginary landscape that holds his own "imprint forever, / and stays unchanged, and waits to be filled back in." After fourteen pages in unmetered verse, this iambic pentameter with one anapestic substitution—the fourth to the last line in the poem—is a rhythmic shock, its meter expressing the permanence and security conveyed in the image.[4] While the semantic and metrical poles of Wright's poem correspond to those of "Quicksand Years," however, the dactyls that drive Wright to pentameter are languid in comparison with Whitman's; his images of wind erasing memory are more poignant than terrifying. Wright's final pentameter image has much in common with the final rhetorical question of "Quicksand Years," "When shows break up what but One's-Self is sure?" But Wright's patiently waiting landscape is a passive vessel for the self, not its active embodiment, and his late-twentieth-century pentameter carries noticeably less self-assertive force than does its predecessor.[5]

Wright's and Whitman's opposing attitudes towards the facility and skill represented by the pentameter are most evident in the passages where Wright's sense of iambic pentameter connotations is closest to Whitman's. In Wright's description of composing poetry in "Journal of the Year of the Ox," for instance, a metrical contrast pairs the idea of superficial poetic facility, embodied prosodically in the pentameter, with the idea of a more authentic or deeply inspired poetry, embodied prosodically in the triple rhythm:

> As I tried to practice my own scales
>   of invisible music
> I thought I heard for hours on a yellow legal pad?
> Verona, I think, the stiff French horn
> Each weekend echoing my own false notes
>   and scrambled lines
> I tried to use as decoys to coax the real things down
> Out of the air they hid in and out of the pencils they hid in . . .

Wright's pentameter conveys conscious poetic effort in contrast to the more ineffable "real thing" hiding in the triple rhythm: "Out of the air they hid in and out of the pencils they hid in." His prosodic dialectic between willed and unwilled poetry is directly in keeping with Whitman's sense of the two metrical patterns. But while one of Whitman's representative metapentameters about literary tradition, "The words of true poems do not merely please," implies that the pentameter needs to be transcended *because* it has been mastered, the words of Wright's pentameter line, "Each weekend echoing my own false notes," imply frustration with the meter for opposite reasons. The horn player's notes are "false" because the musician is a weekend player, not because of facile virtuosity. When Wright's line is read as a comment on its own meter, the poet seems not to be leaving the iambic pentameter behind, but reaching towards it.

Iambic pentameter is not the threat for Wright that it was for poets of the nineteenth and early twentieth centuries; it is a beckoning, while often a faint one. Even when, like Eliot, Wright feels he is drowning in iambic pentameter, its connotations remain positive; as he puts it in the single pentameter in "To Gioacomo Leopardi in the Sky": "How sweet it is to drown in such sure water." Nonetheless, when Wright uses iambic pentameter to express—or to locate—reassurance in physical realities or accepted poetic tradition, he often reveals what one might call, with apologies to Harold Bloom, his metrical belatedness; the iambic pentameters are both more tentative and more resigned than his predecessors' lines in the same connotative cluster. For example, in "Roma 1," bored, alienated lives are grounded and relieved to some extent in a concluding iambic pentameter, the only one in the poem:

> The smell of a dozen dinners is borne up
> On exhaust fumes,
>   timeless, somehow, and vaguely reassuring.

This iambic pentameter's metrical subtext, although consistent with traditional connotations of conventionality, adds only a mild reassurance to the poem's wryly low-key conclusion.

While Wright's use of traditional metrical connotations develops logically from his historical position, it is not the only way that late–twentieth century free-verse poets respond to their metrical inheritance. For Audre Lorde, both iambic pentameter and dactylic rhythms carry abundant stores of wordless energy. Lorde builds on the same metrical connotations and strategies that are evident in Dickinson's poems; like Dickinson, for example, Lorde associates the iambic pentameter with patriarchal restraints. But Lorde's iambic pentameter, through prosodic and verbal techniques, widens the meter's associations so that it expresses a range of emotion from outrage to grief to joy. The significant resources of Lorde's metrical vocabulary are also evident in her frequent and flexible use of the dactylic rhythm, a dramatic expansion on Dickinson's tantalizing handful of dactylic half lines.

Anger in Dickinson's iambic pentameters often surfaces as a sense of defeat, but in Lorde the meter conveys outer-directed rage. Most often, Lorde equates the negative aspects of the iambic pentameter with political and social betrayals, like the symbolic external force in "A Litany for Survival" from Lorde's *The Black Unicorn* (1978):[6]

> for by this weapon
> this illusion of some safety to be found
> the heavy-footed hoped to silence us.

The "illusion" of safety in the first iambic pentameter lures the reader to the encounter with personified cruelty in the second line. Similarly, the only iambic pentameter line in "Equal Opportunity" expresses anger at a black woman's blind collusion with military power:

> The american deputy assistant secretary of defense
> for Equal Opportunity
> and safety
> is a home girl.
> Blindness slashes our tapestry to shreds.

The rage in Lorde's iambic pentameters is not always externalized; in some of her poems the meter expresses an internalized anger which it distances through projection.[7] A statue carries the wounding in two poems inspired by the African goddess Seboulisa, "Dahomey" and "125th Street and Abomey." The only pentameter in the first poem describes a sculpture of the goddess that has "one breast eaten away by worms of sorrow," and the only two pentameters in the second depict "Seboulisa mother goddess with one breast / eaten away by worms of sorrow and loss." In other poems, Lorde's pained iambic pentameters achieve a distancing effect by explicitly mentioning strangers, or by expressing the speaker's sense of alienation from herself: "Out of the storm of strangers and demands" ("Pathways"); "I have died too many deaths / that were not mine" ("Sequelae").[8]

In several poems, Lorde's speaker separates herself from the pain described in iambic pentameters through images of masks and hollowness, which allow the external social causes of pain to approach closer to consciousness. The single iambic pentameter in "Scar," for instance—

> the shape of us at war
> clawing our own flesh out
> to feed the backside of our masklike faces

—describes a smooth surface purchased with great pain; but unlike Dickinson's fully internalized "formal feeling," Lorde's surfaces are clearly artificial and "masklike." The first line and only iambic pentameter in "Eulogy for Alvin Frost," "black men bleeding to death inside themselves," laments hidden internal destruction with another image of a misleading surface.

The flexibility that Lorde's iambic pentameter gains through these semantic devices becomes especially evident in comparison with the approach of her contemporary Judy Grahn, another poet in the metrical-code tradition of Dickinson. Perhaps because Grahn's speaker is more immediately present than Lorde's, Grahn's iambic pentameter in the poem "Like a Woman in Childbirth Wailing" closely resembles some of Dickinson's in its attitude of victimization. Grahn's arrangements of split and iambic pentameters, in particular, show a pattern that correlates with Dickinson's defensive privileging of the canonical meter (see also chap. 2, n. 8). The narrator of Grahn's poem fashions a Dickinsonian progression of split and full pentameters:

> He was so clumsy then
> He tied me up and
> turned me upside down
> to birth against the force of gravity,
> sewing me back together like a doll
> because I ripped, I tore, my organs
> dripped down my legs.

In this passage the split iambic pentameter—"He tied me up and / turned me upside down"—serves only as a semantic stepping-stone to the agonized first full pentameter, "to birth against the force of gravity." While Grahn's poem shows a sensibility akin to Lorde's in its externalized, political anger at the pentameter, it is informed by a split-pentameter configuration that makes the iambic pentameter the goal of the split pentameters as it was for Dickinson. Lorde, by contrast, often opposes the meanings of split pentameters to those of full iambic pentameters. The pattern is clear in each of the three stanzas of "Walking the Boundaries," which contains more iambic pentameters than any other poem in *The Black Unicorn*. In the first stanza of this poem, for example, split-pentameter descriptions of change and decay contrast with two full pentameters describing "one tough missed okra pod cling[ing] to the vine."

Perhaps Lorde's treatment of the split-pentameter pattern is more varied than Grahn's because Lorde has so fully developed the triple rhythm as a prosodic alternative to the pentameter. The dacytlic rhythm functions in her poems as a more accessible, more trustworthy source of poetic power than iambic pentameter; the single dactylic line in "Eulogy for Alvin Frost," for example, describes the speaker's instinctive reach for comfort at news of her colleague's death: "seeking immediate ground for my feet to embrace."

Like Whitman, Crane, Eliot, and Charles Wright, Lorde associates the triple rhythm with the ineffable and with nature. But for Lorde, this metrical pattern carries no connotations of terrifying, sad, or even poignant chaos. Lorde treats the triple rhythm as a positive, natural female force, as does Dickinson in her rare and brief dactyls. Lorde tends to funnel the energy of the triple rhythm into erotic lines like these from "Woman": "moonstone and ebony opal / giving milk to all of my hungers," or these from "Meet": "tasting your ruff down to sweetness . . . Come in the curve of the lion's bulging stomach / lie for a season out of the judging rain." In "Scar," erotic joy extends into an imagined community of women who are

> learning the dance of open and closing
> learning a dance of electrical tenderness
> no father no mother would teach them.[9]

On occasion Lorde, like Whitman, uses the iambic pentameter and the triple rhythm to one rhetorical end. At the end of "Dahomey," she writes,

> Bearing two drums on my head I speak
> whatever language is needed
> to sharpen the knives of my tongue.

The passage, consisting of a headless iambic pentameter and two lines in triple rhythm, metrically echoes its stated conviction to speak in more than one language. The central line, describing the speaker's willingness to accomodate her rhythms to the occasion, is the most metrically ambiguous of the three and essentially combines both rhythms; it is not until after the word "language" that it becomes clear that this line is not iambic. Lorde also combines both rhythms in "Chain." Here a single iambic pentameter describes the bodies of two girls, victims of incest, imagined as lying on the speaker's porch. The commonsense tone of the line draws on the pentameter's connotation of objective reliability to make the speaker's vision convincing: "I cannot step past them nor over them." Then the two lines in dactylic rhythm counter the objectivity, addressing the reader's emotions with private images and strong feelings: "Which mirror to break or mourn?"; "Winter has come and the children are dying."

In certain poems like the long poem "Outside," the connotations that the pentameter carries metamorphose because of the dactylic rhythm. Here, the iambic pentameters change their tone after one line of triple rhythm in the middle of the poem. As the first stanza opens, the pentameter describes an alienating, powerful world, distanced with anger: "In the center of a harsh and spectrumed city . . . I grew up in a genuine confusion." The second stanza opens with a single dactylic line that, like the image of feet reaching for the ground in "Eulogy for Alvin Frost," shows the poet searching for comfort through communion with her own truth: "And how many times have I called myself back." In the next pentameter, at the resolution of "Outside," the meter has become important to the called-back self and, we can assume, to the speaker's identity as a poet: "and I am lustful now for my own name." Lorde has transformed the tone of the pentameter through contact with the elemental feelings described in the triple rhythm. By the poem's conclusion, with the lines,

and I am blessed within my selves
who are come to make our shattered faces
whole,

the final split iambic pentameter has taken on a healing, redemptive power.

In both Lorde's and Dickinson's work, anger at the pentameter and exhiliration at claiming its authority engender much poetic energy. For Dickinson, the canonical meter is a fixed entity whose power cannot be altered, but only accepted or rejected. The dilemma that this situation produces is a remarkably, and sometimes excruciatingly, fertile source of tension in her poetry. Lorde's historical position offers a wider range of approaches to iambic pentameter than were available to Dickinson. In poems like "Outside," Lorde transforms the connotations of iambic pentameter as much as she inherits them. Furthermore, although the fact that Lorde writes in dactyls owes much to Whitman, Crane, and Eliot, her associations to the triple rhythm depart from those in previous poetry. Both Lorde and Wright emerge from the midcentury hiatus with a new attitude towards metrical connotations. But Lorde follows a less fully formed tradition than Wright, and her metrical practice carries as strong an undercurrent of discovery as his does of nostalgia.

Notes

Chapter 1

1. More than one writer has noted the possibility of the metrical code, but none has developed it explicitly at length. Dennis Taylor mentions the metrical code in his book on Hardy's meter: "I . . . assume that a traditional line may carry with it associations which remain when the line is combined with other types of lines in a complex stanza" (77–78). Gingell, analyzing how the Canadian poet A. M. Klein uses versification "to reinforce thematic statement" (15), notes that Klein used individual lines of iambic pentameter to evoke the British poetic tradition.

2. A fourth theory about meter and meaning, which may be called *artifice*—the idea that poems gain a level of meaning from the mere fact of their metricality—has been mentioned by twentieth-century theorists including I. A. Richards, Victor Hamm, and Paul Fussell. Richards noted in 1925 that meter sets a poem apart "through its very appearance of artificiality" (*Principles* 145). Fussell summarizes the artifice theory as the idea that "meter, by distinguishing rhythmic from ordinary statement, objectifies that statement and impels it in the direction of a significant formality and even ritualism" (*Poetic Meter* 14). Hamm writes that meter "has a meaning, if only the meaning of an established order" (700). The artifice theory may be too general for any theorist to discuss at length, although it influenced Hollander's development of the frame theory (*Vision* 135–36).

Overviews of the relation between meter and meaning usually emphasize the iconic and frame theories. Szerdahelyi, for example, distinguishes between the two ideas by borrowing Charles Pierce's concepts of symbol and icon: meter functions as an iconic sign when it imitates the phenomena the poem describes, and as a symbolic sign when it "evoke[s] in us the atmosphere, feelings and ideals of the world in which it . . . originated and flourished." The hexameter, for instance, evokes classical culture (80–81). Tarlinskaja concentrates on the iconic theory, demonstrating in detail how "deviations" from the general metrical model of the text may "perform the function of italics emphasizing words semantically valuable for the poet or . . . functionally approach sound imitation, iconically reproducing kinetic or acoustic images" (1–2). She also describes an association exemplifying the frame theory in her discussion of "historical" connections between form and meaning: "trochaic trimeter rhymed feminine-masculine-feminine-masculine is strongly associated in the Russian literary tradition with the theme "unhappy childhood or death in a rural setting" (1).

3. With the benefit of hindsight, a modern scholar such as Raven can imply, on the other hand, that the Greeks used anapestic meter when there was movement on the stage because it was traditionally a marching meter (11).

4. At least one writer of antiquity did apply the iconic theory as well as the propriety theory. Johnson notes that Dionysius of Halicarnassus in the first century B.C. described how Homer's hexameters expressed "length of time, bulk of body, . . . brevity, speed," and other characteristics "by the sound of the syllables" (*De Compositione Verborum*, trans. and qtd. in Johnson, *Rambler* 123). Johnson is skeptical of Dionysius' claims: "either he was fanciful, or we have lost the genuine pronounciation" (*Rambler* 124).

5. Late in the chapter, Hall verges on the iconic theory in his remark that Shakespeare made an "intuitive choice of precisely those rhythmic regularities and irregularities which could best express his emotion and his thought" (44). He supports this claim, however, with only a half paragraph of general discussion: "the reversal [trochaic substitution] . . . startles us and charms," "consecutive stresses [spondees] . . . give a refreshing variety, and slow the march of thought," and "omitted stresses . . . give rapidity and fluidity to a line" (44–45). In each of these instances, an emphasis on aesthetic appeal ("charms," "refreshing," "fluidity") tempers the discussion of iconic function with aesthetic considerations.

6. For a general critique of the claims of stylistics, please see Fish.

7. Both essays are now included in Hollander's *Vision and Resonance*. In related work, Greenblatt discusses how "genre can exert a powerful influence on the metrical stylistic feature of complexity" (23). He finds that Donne and Jonson, for instance, use high levels of substitution for the expected metrical pattern in their satires, very low levels in house poems and funeral elegies, and a middle range in love poems. Not only particular generic traditions but the influence of individual poets have been found to affect metrical associations; Kenneth Gross finds that Mil-

ton's use of the hexameter reflects a consciousness of Spenser's previous associations with the line.

Chapter 2

1. Among those who have discussed Dickinson's hymn stanza, see especially Thomas Johnson 84–120; Whicher 165–69, 240–42; Porter 51–74; Wolosky 14–17; and Lindberg-Seyersted 129–56, 161–62.

2. Joanne Feit Diehl develops the idea in her book *Dickinson and the Romantic Imagination* (esp. 7–10, 13–33, and 82–83) and in her article "Dickinson and Bloom."

3. Clark Griffin calls this tactic "the cruellest kind of irony" (66).

4. See Gilbert and Gubar, *Madwoman* 587–94; Juhasz, *Naked* 13, 31; Mossberg, esp. 74–82; and Cheryl Walker 87–94, 109–11, for discussions of Dickinson in relation to other female "singers" of the time. The idea of Dickinson's intimate consciousness of the object is interestingly developed in Homans ("Oh, Vision") and in Wolosky 165–66.

5. By contrast, Barton Levi St. Armand has a valuable and original explanation of Dickinson's use of the hymn stanza. He discusses her as a folk poet and her poems as "art hymns," exploring the connection between this aspect of her work and various contemporaneous art forms (158–60).

6. Ruth Miller argues that Dickinson may very well have read Whitman in spite of this claim (65–67). See also Keller 251–93. For further discussion of Dickinson in relation to other writers see Sewall 1:678; Whicher 214–16; and Capps 23–24, 60–66, 83–92, 113–15, 134–35. Dickinson even sewed a sampler with an iambic-pentameter poem in 1845 (Leyda 1:99). Dickinson's resistance to iambic pentameter is still more remarkable in the light of Bogus's view that an "ingested remembrance of Elizabeth Barrett Browning as teacher" is "at the heart of Dickinson's poetics" (44) and Walsh's claim that Dickinson borrowed extensively from Barrett Browning (98–109). Vivian Pollak's article on the valentines Dickinson wrote shows that she was both knowledgeable and ambivalent about the Augustan poetic conventions, parodying the forms and attitudes that most attracted her.

7. I base my criteria for the metricality of a ten-syllable line on Halle and Keyser, as follows:

> inverted feet [trochees] appear only under the following three conditions in an iambic pentameter line: verse initially, after a stressed syllable..., and after a major syntactic boundary ... across which the subordination rules of English do not operate. (231)

Babette Deutsch claims that "a trochee might be substituted for an iamb anywhere save in the final foot" (*Poetry Handbook 88*), including, apparently, after pyrrhic substitutions. A looser definition than either of these might be appropriate, however, in view of Hollander's remark that a

> metrical loan from the poetry of another language always tends to show up, in the borrowing tongue, as an inscriptional coding: consider the pure syllabics from the French . . . first used by Marianne Moore and W. H. Auden . . . one cannot scan them by ear, but only by counting one's fingers. (*Vision* 251)

One might see the male poetic tradition as "another language," and certain irregular pentameters as examples of an "abstract . . . visual meter" (*Vision* 251), not completely natural to Dickinson's ear.

    8. Often the split iambic-pentameter lines are apologetic or defensive in meaning, inadequate as they are in relation to the canonical meter: "Bear with the Ballad— / Awkward—faltering" (poem 1059); "Hate cannot harm / A Foe so reticent—" (poem 1356). These lines seem to imply that iambic pentameter is an ideal standard. The relation is clear in these lines from poem 1109, which contain one full and then one split iambic pentameter:

> A purer food for them, if I succeed,
> If not I had
> The transport of the Aim—.

Since the canonical meter both empowers and disempowers, however, it is not surprising that Dickinson presents some split iambic pentameters as defeats because they resemble iambic pentameter rather than because they depart from it:

> When I have lost, you'll know by this—
> A Bonnet black—A dusk surplice—
> A little tremor in my voice
> Like this! (poem 104);

"Papa above! / Regard a Mouse / O'erpowered by the Cat!" (poem 61).

    9. Dickinson's metrical frugality demonstrates yet another aspect of her frequently noted poetic parsimoniousness (other aspects are her withholding of information and her unwillingness to provide syntactical connections and conventional punctuation) and of the paradoxical richness and strength her poetry derives from this attitude. See especially Eberwein's essay and book; Kammer; Cristanne Miller; Whicher 235–37; Pearce 175–77; and Lindberg-Seyersted 22, 234–37. The following quotations are representative: "In her experience, the wren positioned herself more strategically than the giant" (Eberwein, *Dickinson* 20), "Privation is more plentiful than plenty" (Wilbur 38), "Renunciation is a way to say no, and as such it puts power suddenly in the hands of the previously powerless" (Juhasz, *Undiscovered* 174).

Chapter 3

1. Swinburne wrote this essay after abandoning his earlier enthusiasm for Whitman. The passage in question is worth quoting in full:

But metre, rhythm, cadence not merely appreciable but definable and reducible to rule and measurement, though we do not expect from you, we demand from all who claim, we discern in the works of all who have achieved, any place among poets of any class whatsoever. The question whether your work is in any sense poetry has no more to do with dulcet rhymes than with the differential calculus. The question is whether you have any more right to call yourself a poet, or to be called a poet by any man who knows verse from prose, or black from white, or speech from silence, or his right hand from his left, than to call yourself or to be called, on the strength of your published writings, a mathematician, a logician, a painter, a political economist, a sculptor, a dynamiter, an old parliamentary hand, a civil engineer, a dealer in marine stores, an amphimacer, a triptych, a rhomboid, or a rectangular parallelogram. "Vois-tu bien, tu es baron comme ma pantoufle!" said old Gillenormand [in *Les Miserables*]—the creature of one who was indeed a creator or a poet: and the humblest of critics who knows any one thing from any one other thing has a right to say to the man who offers as poetry what the exuberant incontinence of a Whitman presents for our acceptance, "Tu es poete comme mon—soulier." (202)

2. Those who have pointed out the rarity of actual dactyls in Whitman include Harvey Gross, who claims that "the scansion of stressed and unstressed syllables has no relevance to Whitman's prosody," while conceding that "occasionally Whitman's lines fall into scannable hexameters" (83–84), and Gay Wilson Allen, who remarks in his *New Walt Whitman Handbook* that "most of Whitman's poems contain occasional lines that scan easily as iambic, trochaic, anapestic, or—very rarely—dactylic" (241). Additional writers on the other side of the question include Basil de Selincourt ("the hexameter is quite a favorite [line in Whitman]" [66]), and Anthony Burgess ("His basic rhythm is an epic one—the Virgilian dactyl-spondee—and his line often hexametric" [48]). In "The Maligning of Walt Whitman," Felix Stefanile credits Whitman for his "versatile, and old-fashioned metrical virtuosity," and scans the opening of "Out of the Cradle Endlessly Rocking" as "an interplay of dactyls and trochees that proceeds, with finesse and modulation, throughout the whole glorious work" (8). Esther Shephard notes that Whitman changed the wording of the prose passage from which he derived "To the Man-of-War Bird" "in order to create a rhythm which

is composed, roughly, of dactyls and trochees" (49). Saintsbury heard "confused echoes of Evangeline hexameters" in Whitman (*History* 492).

3. Paul Fussell, *Theory of Prosody in Eighteenth Century England* 140. See also "A Note on Samuel Johnson and the Rise of Accentual Prosodic Theory," which shows that even Johnson, the most conservative of prosodists, became aware of the rising tendency toward accentualism between the 1755 and 1773 editions of the *Dictionary*.

4. In "The Rationale of Verse" Poe sets out his own prosodic theory, involving time equivalences, which can account for his syllabic freedoms without recourse to Bryant's idea of foot substitution. Whatever its justification, however, Poe's use of triple rhythms, both alone and in combination with duple rhythms, fed and encouraged the hunger for triple meters in the American ear. Saintsbury has noted "reminiscences" of Poe and Longfellow in Whitman ("Review of *Leaves of Grass*" 789; also see n. 2 above). James Wright discusses Whitman's respect for Longfellow in "The Delicacy of Walt Whitman" (163–64).

5. For this last explanation, I am grateful to Paul Kiparsky of Stanford University. The relation of the rise of triple meters to the development of free verse is discussed more fully in the next chapter.

6. The most conspicuous difference between the two poets' ways of opposing the canonical meter, the fact that Dickinson shortened the pentameter line and Whitman lengthened it, relates to two ideas discussed in chapter 2: Dickinson's choice of a well-established as opposed to an anarchic meter, and the renunciative aspect of her poetics explored by Eberwein and others. For an example of the connotative meaning of Dickinson's hymn stanza, see the first stanza of poem 1677 ("On my volcano grows the grass"), discussed on pages 22–23 of this book.

7. Whitman also refers to democracy in an iambic pentameter in "Thou Mother With Thy Equal Brood": "Sail, sail thy best, ship of democracy," and in the embedded iambic pentameter that concludes "The Commonplace": "The democratic wisdom underneath, like solid ground for all." One explanation for the metrical contradiction here is that these pentameters reflect a less mystical and grandiose, and perhaps a less threatening, view of democracy than do the dactylic lines.

8. In reference to this identification of a poem's poem-ness with the poet's literary self-assertion, John Hollander has observed, in a discussion of a Wordsworth sonnet, that even the phrase "'work of art' can confuse the making with the thing made, the being-in-and-at the sonnet with the poem or the paradigm of the poem itself" (*Melodious Guile* 88).

9. Basically the systematic theories of Whitman's prosody can be divided into accentual theories, syntactic theories, and phrase-unit theories; nonsystematic opinions are also common. In the first group, Hindus

sees the typical line in Whitman as a three-beat measure, and Robert Cory, as four isochronous beats. In the second group, Andrew Schiller concentrates, as does Allen in *American Prosody,* on isosyntactical patterning, and Ross sees the prosody as determined by "units of sense" (364). In the third group, Rosemary Gates develops a theory of phonological phrases with expressive rhythmic patterns, and for Scott the line simply "consists, like the prose sentence, of an advancing and retreating wave" (152). A representative nonsystematic opinion is Muriel Rukeyser's remark that Whitman's prosody was based on spontaneous physical knowledge rather than on any literary associations: "[Whitman] remembered his body as other poets of his time remembered English verse" (105–6). Matthiessen also discusses Whitman's "discovery of the physical grounding of rhythm," noting how it differs from Coleridge's idea of meter as the tension between emotion and its control (567). These theories are generally ahistorical except insofar as they note Whitman's relation to biblical syntax.

10. James E. Miller points out that Whitman's friends have done him more harm "by their comparisons with Christ" than have his enemies by their various criticisms.

Chapter 4

1. Strangely enough in view of Crane's poetry, two of his acquaintances compared him to Poe and made no mention of Whitman. Robert Barr wrote, "I always fancied that Edgar Allan Poe revisited the earth as S. Crane, trying again, succeeding again, failing again." (Crane, *Letters* 286–87), and Hamlin Garland remarked of Crane that "it seems now that he was destined from the first to be a sort of present-day Poe" (Crane, *Letters* 305).

2. Summing up the conflicting qualities in poetry of Crane's time in general, Duffey has called it the "poetry of incoherence" (154).

3. Even scholars who were not part of either the romantic movement or the revival of hexameters were cognizant of a change in the texture of verse. James Morgan Hart, for instance, described in 1884 his reluctance to teach contemporary poetry, based on his "suspicion that we are at this moment living in a new period, which has just begun and which is slowly and unconsciously evolving something, the precise shape of which no one foresees" (90). Hart describes how his own taste in verse has changed: on first reading Byron's *Manfred* and *Cain,* he found the meter "halting and defective. This was probably because it had not the flow that I was used to." Subsequent reading convinced him that Byron's blank verse "at its best was inferior to nothing in Shakespeare or Mil-

ton." In order to arrive at this conclusion, Hart had developed new semiotic habits anticipating the iconic theory:

> Observe how seldom [Byron's] pauses fall full and sonorous, how the caesura seems to vacillate. Unlike Shakespeare pouring forth his passion, unlike Milton sublime in his confidence, Byron has to insinuate his doubts and cavils. And the metre sympathizes with this mood. . . . It is . . . the first signal example of the blank verse of doubt and misgiving. (94–95)

4. Southey, in his 1821 "Preface" to *A Vision of Judgement,* explained as follows:

> the trochee has been substituted for the spondee, as by the Germans. This substitution is rendered necessary by the nature of our pronounciation, which is so rapid, that I believe the whole vocabulary of the language does not afford a single instance of a genuine native spondee. (425)

Southey goes on to say that the only true spondee in English is the word *Egypt.* For a discussion of the same phenomenon a century later, see Bridges, who feels that the impossibility of spondees precludes English hexameters (94). The view still generally held is that stress is so essential a part of English that of any two successive syllables, one will in most cases be stressed slightly more than the other. Nabokov calls it "sheer lunacy" to see "Rise! Rise," for example, as a spondee, since in a poem "the force of the meter sorts out the monosyllables in a certain, iambic way" (28). But Winters admits spondees in rare kinds of heavily accented verse (139), and the *Princeton Encyclopedia of Poetry and Poetics* accepts compound words and adjacent monosyllables as English spondees (808). Linguist Paul Kiparsky, in an unpublished comment, sums up the question as "purely terminological (do we want spondee to refer to a foot with two stresses? Or with two equal stresses?)."

5. Tsur, incidentally, points out that the feeling of anxiety is emphasized in this line of Milton's because, in terms of the Halle-Keyser theory, "*bot-* is a stress maximum in a weak position" (425).

6. In "The Rationale of Verse," Poe offers one sensible explanation for the fact that English hexameters of the period were so often thought to sound like prose. Using some lines of *Evangeline* as an example, Poe shows that they are much longer than classical hexameters, since they are composed almost completely of dactyls while the classical dactylic hexameter was in fact primarily spondaic. Poe finally reprints the Longfellow lines with all the feet in "their proper position," so that they make "respectable prose" (264). The idea that all the additional syllables make the lines seem more prosaic is additional evidence for Weissmuller's idea that the strong-stress principle led accentual-syllabic verse towards prose

(see pages 65–66 of this book), since more unstressed syllables would emphasize the strength of the dactylic stresses.

7. In his essay on Longfellow, Dana Gioia describes the definitive reaction against triple meter as having taken place during the twentieth century:

Twentieth century American poetry has gradually developed a metrical puritanism, a conviction among both poets and critics that serious formal poetry is best written . . . only in regular or loose iambics. Triple and trochaic meters have gradually been relegated to light verse, classical and foreign meters regarded as technical curiosities. This metrical puritanism developed as second-generation Modernists, many of whom like Yvor Winters and Allen Tate were associated with New Criticism, tried to reconcile formal metrics with Modernism. In the process of defending traditional meter against free verse, they felt it necessary to separate the meters suitable for high art from the catchy tunes of popular poetry. The tightness and subtlety of iambic meters were preferred to the intrusive and looser rhythms of triple meter or the hypnotic but inflexible trochaic measures.

Several decades of free verse may have made the job of these twentieth-century critics easier; how much more obtrusive an isoaccentual line sounds to an ear accustomed only to free verse.

Gioia's account of the twentieth-century attempt to reinstate metrical verse by repressing one of the two prosodic contenders is consistent with Martin Halpern's and Edward Weissmuller's theory that free verse results from an impasse or confusion between them, discussed on pages 65–66 of this book.

8. Ed Folsom notes that at least ten sonnets addressed to Whitman were published in the mid–nineteenth century (xxvi).

9. Paul Kiparsky, in an unpublished comment, defines Whitman's characteristic measure as being "in the spirit of the dolnik"—a mixed meter consisting of two- and three-syllable rising rhythms.

10. While Crane was not typical in the metrical forms his disillusionment took, his disenchantment with the ideal of progress and the values of his era was representative. See Robert Walker 200, 231, 284 for parallels between Crane's attitudes and those of other poets of his day.

11. As support for this scanning-from-the-end method, I offer not only my own ear but an unpublished remark of Dana Gioia, who also employs the technique: "it is easier to begin a line in [metrical] ambiguity than to end it in ambiguity."

12. In order to emphasize the rhythms relevant to this book's argument, I have not made use of possible other feet such as the amphibrach ($\cup\prime\cup$), cretic ($\prime\cup\prime$), or first paeon ($\prime\cup\cup\cup$) in the Crane scansions.

13. Or as spondaic as possible. See n. 4 of this chapter for views on the possibility of spondees in English.

Chapter 5

1. The popular conception seems otherwise in a 1950 *Time* magazine profile which speaks of Eliot's poetic predictability as matter-of-factly as if Alexander Pope were the poet under discussion: "As precisely as an Eliot rhyme clicking into place, 4 o'clock each day brings tea with friends or business acquaintances" ("Reflections" 26).

2. Some critics have dealt with the problem by using completely different prosodic conventions in order to read Eliot. See, for example, Hewitt, who emphasizes speech cadence in her reading of "Ash Wednesday," and Freedman, who hears jazz rhythms in Eliot's poetry. Levy makes an interesting analysis of Eliot's basic meter as loose, quasi-Websterian blank verse, disguised and confused by the frequent enjambment which emphasizes sentence syntax instead of the line.

3. For more on Eliot's concept of verse and prose, see Costello 14–37 and *passim.*

4. That reputation was so immense for at least one generation of American poets that, as Howard Nemerov puts it in his description of being reduced to giggles in front of his students at the prospect of having to teach *Four Quartets,* "for many years . . . I had looked on these poems as on The Word" (57). Hugh Kenner notes the almost uncanny appeal of Eliot's poetic voice: "certainly no other modern verses so invade the mind" (4).

5. The roots are, of course, evident much earlier, if one considers Arnold's irregular verse, Tennyson's accentual prosody, Robert Browning's speech patterns, and romantic ideas of organic form.

6. Examples are discussed on page 33 of this book.

7. Soldo finds many echoes of Laforgue in Eliot's early work, and Babette Deutsch notes several passages in Eliot that paraphrase Laforgue, as well as echoes of Mallarmé and Gautier (*Poetry in Our Time* 170–73). Also see Svarny 44–64. Leavis qualifies the influence of Laforgue on Eliot's verse technique as follows: "French moves so differently from English that to learn from French verse an English poet must be strongly original. And to learn as Mr. Eliot learnt in general from Laforgue is to be original to the point of genius" (79).

8. By contrast, Boughn argues that Richard Aldington and John Gould Fletcher could not prevent their free verse from falling into regular accentual-syllabic metrical patterns (113–14).

9. For more detailed treatment of this subject, see the discussion of Weissmuller's ideas on pages 65–66 of this book.

10. Hughes cites the classical scholar Henry Rushton Fairclough on the Hellenism of H.D.'s style: "In his opinion the sort of free verse which she employs is admirably suited to the rendering of Greek lyrics" (118). Stauffer notes that Masters modeled his first free-verse *Spoon River Anthology* poems on the epigrams in *The Greek Anthology,* which a friend gave him in 1909 (245).

11. By 1916, free verse was also ready to be parodied; in that year Witter Bynner and Arthur Davison Ficke passed off a book of fake imagist verse, *Spectra,* as the work of "newly discovered free verse poets," and the joke became "the talk of the literary season" (Gregory 185).

12. Henry B. Fuller makes the same connection between free verse and the jaded contemporary taste, without Eastman's condescension, in an article that has no intention of attacking vers libre:

But a lively, over-driven, urban body of readers, limited as to time and harried by an appetite for novel notions, should welcome the new vehicle [i.e., free verse]; the sort of reader who nibbles, sips, flirts his napkin, twitches his chair, looks down the board and asks, "What next?" He is the devotee—or the victim—of the quick tempo; he hears the end before the end is reached and is already preparing to ask for another tune. (516)

13. See Steele 66–67 for more on Eliot's and Williams's disillusionment with free verse.

14. Several years later, a remark by Robert Graves notes even more conclusively the extent to which free verse had been established in America:

The history of American poetry is not to be compared with our own. Walt Whitman's free verse has become classically legitimised, and it is no sign of particular rebelliousness to prefer his example to that of Longfellow. Miss Amy Lowell's polyphonics, for instance, are almost haughtily traditional: if she were an Englishwoman she would certainly be writing in strict metres. (7)

15. Rees notes of this stanza, "The monotonously insistent duple rhythms of the fourth stanza match the dreary monotony of Prufrock's meditations" (54).

16. One can speculate that if Eliot had found his meta–free verse as authoritative as Whitman's metapentameter, he might have written as much in strict pentameter as Whitman wrote in free verse.

17. Perhaps the choice of pentameter here is conditioned by the romanticism that Lobb sees in Eliot's aesthetic: "Eliot partakes . . . of another aspect of the Romantic sensibility—the tendency to look *back* to a source of value" (62).

18. Throughout my reading of *The Waste Land,* I have relied on Gish for various explanations of allusions as well as for translations of non-English passages.

19. Like the transformation out of the Shakespeare-based passage in the dressing-room scene, the transformation out of a Spenser-based passage here happens at a line based on a subsequent poet—in this case, Marvell instead of Milton. In each case, the line that seems to effect the transformation is longer by a foot than its model—a hexameter for the Milton pentameter, a pentameter for the Marvell tetrameter. Perhaps the act of adding the extra foot leads to a sense of random pointlessness, which in turn finds expression in the subsequent images of despair.

20. Other writers who have noted Whitman's influence on Eliot include Harvey Gross 84, Bloom, "Introduction" 2, Hartman 121–23, and Edwin Fussell 144–45.

21. For an explanation of my use of the term *dactylic* here and elsewhere, see pages 39–40 of this book.

22. Interestingly, Gregory S. Jay finds that insofar as it allegorizes the reader's encounter with the text, the "compound ghost" passage recalls Whitman's "Song of Myself" (110). One of the functions of the pentameter here might be to keep the Whitmanic influence at bay.

Chapter 6

1. See Middlebrook 20–21, 48, 51 for a discussion of Sexton's early experience writing metrical verse.

2. During this time schoolchildren were also encouraged to write poetry in free verse, as they were during the first wave of vers libre. See, for example, Koch. For a discussion of the earlier vogue for free verse, see pages 92–93 of this book.

3. The second line, of course, has ten syllables. but according to Halle and Keyser it cannot be scanned as an iambic pentameter since the trochee in the third foot follows a pyrrhic. Even if one argues that the pyrrhic is actually an iamb, since the word "and" would get more weight than the second syllable of "finite," I would still argue that the line has a strong dactylic swing after the opening unstressed syllable, particularly in contrast to the decisive iambic movement of the preceding line, which is strong enough to take the anapestic substitution in the second foot in stride with hardly a falter. And of course, any initial ambiguity in sensing the triple rhythm of the second line perfectly embodies the idea that the spirit/flesh difference is only "slowly transgressable."

4. The other pentameters in the poem appear at the beginning, and in meaning they convey a sense of betrayal like that which led Eliot to

abandon the pentameter during the course of *The Waste Land*. For example, in these lines an early identity disappears; the ocean is "brooding and self-absorbed"; it deals a random poker hand of blank cards. This line reclaims the meter from such ambivalence.

5. A reading of "Quicksand Years" appears on pages 40–41 of this book.

6. All of Lorde's poems referred to in this chapter are from *The Black Unicorn*.

7. An occasional three-line split pentameter hides the most direct expressions of internalized anger; "Portrait," for example, opens with the lines "Strong women / know the taste / of their own hatred." Another three-line split pentameter at the end of "Dream/Songs From the Moon of Beulah Land" explains the reining in of iambic pentameter force at these times of intense pain: "If I ever really sounded / I would rupture / your eardrums / or your heart."

8. A particular kind of distanced personal pain unites a surprisingly coherent group of Lorde's iambic pentameters that describe alienation, not from strangers, but from the speaker's mother. The meter invokes the mother in the context of several anecdotes within long meditative poems on race and childhood. In a poem called "Pathways: From Mother to Mother," the speaker, "imprisoned in the pews of memory," remembers her mother's "bloody wisdom / pewed oracular and seminal as rape." In "Bazaar," the pentameters describe her as "bound in the skin of my mother / anxious and ugly as a lump of iron." In "Sequelae," the split pentameter "I have died too many deaths / that were not mine" distances the speaker from the painful memories of childhood with her mother, expressed in two full pentameters: "seductive as the pain of voiceless mornings / . . . cornflakes shrieking like banshees in my throat," lines which apparently respond to a fear expressed elsewhere in the poem of "becoming my mother."

9. Significantly, one of Lorde's very few negative dactylic connotations, which occurs in a split triple rhythm passage, describes the pain caused by the same erotic fusion and loss of boundaries in a case of unrequited love: "the words became sabers / cutting my boundaries /to ribbons / of merciless light" ("Dream/Songs From the Moon of Beulah Land").

Bibliography of Works Cited

Aiken, Conrad. "An Anatomy of Melancholy." *T. S. Eliot: The Man and His Work*. Ed. Allen Tate. New York: Delacorte Press, 1966. 194–202.

Allen, Gay Wilson. *American Prosody*. New York: American Book Co., 1935.

———. *The New Walt Whitman Handbook*. New York: New York University Press, 1975.

Antrim, Harry T. *T. S. Eliot's Concept of Language: A Study of Its Development*. Gainesville: University of Florida Press, 1971.

Aristotle. "Poetics." Trans. Ingram Bywater. *Introduction to Aristotle*. 2d ed. Ed. Richard McKeon. Chicago: University of Chicago Press, 1973. 661–713.

Arnold, Matthew. *On Translating Homer*. 1905. Ed. W. H. D. Rouse. New York: AMS Press, 1971.

Auden, W. H. *Collected Poems*. Ed. Edward Mendelson. New York: Random, 1976.

Barry, Sister M. Martin. *An Analysis of the Prosodic Structure of Selected Poems of T. S. Eliot*. Washington: Catholic University of America Press, 1948.

Barthes, Roland. *The Grain of the Voice*. Trans. Linda Coverdale. New York: Hill and Wang, 1985.

———. *Mythologies*. Trans. Annette Lavers. New York: Hill and Wang, 1972.

———. *S/Z*. Trans. Richard Howard. New York: Hill and Wang, 1974.

Benson, Carl. "Short Chapters on Novel and Exotic Meters. Chapter 1. The Hexameter and the Pentameter." *American Review: A Whig Journal* 4 (1846): 482–85.

Berryman, John. *Stephen Crane*. American Men of Letters Series. New York: Sloane, 1950.

Blake, William. *Milton*. Boulder, Colorado: Shambala, 1978.

Bloom, Harold. *The Anxiety of Influence*. London: Oxford University Press, 1973.

———. "Introduction." *T. S. Eliot*. Ed. Harold Bloom. New York: Chelsea House, 1985. 1–7.

Bly, Robert. *American Poetry: Wildness and Domesticity*. New York: Harper and Row, 1990.

Bodenheim, Maxwell. "A Reply to A. C. H." *Poetry* 14, no. 3 (June 1919): 170–73.

Bogan, Louise. "The Pleasures of Formal Poetry." *The Poet's Work*. Ed. Reginald Gibbons. Boston: Houghton, 1979. 203–14.

Bogus, S. Diane. "Not So Disparate: An Investigation of the Influence of Elizabeth Barrett Browning on the Work of Emily Dickinson." *Dickinson Studies* 49 (1984): 38–45.

Boughn, Michael. "Elements of the Sounding: H.D. and the Origins of Modernist Prosodies." *Sagetrieb* 6, no. 2 (1987): 101–22.

Bradley, Sculley. "The Fundamental Metrical Principle in Whitman's Poetry." *American Literature* 10 (1939): 437–59.

Brewer, R. F. *The Art of Versification and the Technicalities of Poetry*. Edinburgh: John Grant, 1931.

Bridges, Robert. *Milton's Prosody: With a Chapter on Accentual Verse and Notes*. 1921. Oxford: Oxford University Press, 1967.

Brooks, Cleanth, and Robert Penn Warren. *Understanding Poetry: An Anthology for College Students*. 1938. New York: Henry Holt, 1953.

Browne, William Hand. "Certain Considerations Touching the Structure of English Verse." *MLN* 4 (1889): 193–202.

Bryant, William Cullen. "On the Use of Trisyllabic Feet in Iambic Verse." *North American Review* 9 (1819): 426–31.

Burgess, Anthony. *Urgent Copy*. New York: Norton, 1968.

Cady, Edwin H. *Stephen Crane*. Boston: Twayne Publishers, 1980.

Capps, Jack L. *Emily Dickinson's Reading: 1836–1886*. Cambridge: Harvard University Press, 1966.

Chalker, John. "Aspects of Rhythm and Rhyme in Eliot's Early Poems." *English* 16 (1966): 84–88.

Clark, Suzanne. "The Unwarranted Discourse: Sentimental Community, Modernist Women, and the Case of Millay." *Genre* 20, no. 2 (1987): 133–52.

Clive, Arthur. "The Trammels of Poetic Expression." *The Gentleman's Magazine* n.s. 14 (1875): 184–97.

Cory, Robert E. "The Prosody of Walt Whitman." *North Dakota Quarterly* 28 (1968): 74–79.

Costello, Sister Mary Cleophas. *Between Fixity and Flux: A Study of the Concept of Poetry in the Criticism of T. S. Eliot*. Washington: Catholic University of America Press, 1947.

Crane, Stephen. *The Complete Poems of Stephen Crane*. Ed. Joseph Katz. Ithaca: Cornell University Press, 1972.

———. *Stephen Crane: Letters*. Ed. R. W. Stallman and Lillian Gilkes. New York: New York University Press, 1960.

Crombie, Winifred. *Free Verse and Prose Styles*. London: Croom Helm, 1987.

Cunningham, J. V. *The Collected Essays of J. V. Cunningham*. Chicago: Swallow, 1976.

De Selincourt, Basil. *Walt Whitman: A Critical Study*. London: Martin Secker, 1914.

Dell, Floyd. "A Winged Word." *Poetry* 6, no. 6 (Sept. 1915): 319–20.

Deutsch, Babette. *Poetry Handbook*. New York: Grosset, 1962.

————. *Poetry in Our Time: A Critical Survey of Poetry in the English-speaking World 1900 to 1960.* 2d ed. Garden City: Doubleday, 1963.

Dickinson, Emily. *The Complete Poems of Emily Dickinson.* Ed. Thomas H. Johnson. Cambridge: Harvard University Press, 1955.

————. *The Letters of Emily Dickinson.* Ed. Thomas H. Johnson and Theodora Ward. 3 vols. Cambridge: Harvard University Press, 1958.

Diehl, Joanne Feit. "Dickinson and Bloom: An Antithetical Reading of Romanticism." *Texas Studies in Literature and Language* 23 (1981): 418–41.

————. *Dickinson and the Romantic Imagination.* Princeton: Princeton University Press, 1981.

Diering, F. K. "Metre and Meaning." *Crux,* December 1985, 35–41.

Dowden, Edward. "The Poet of Democracy: Walt Whitman." *Studies in Literature.* London: Keegan Paul, Trench, Trubner and Co., 1878. Rpt. in Woodress 99–108.

Duffey, Bernard. *Poetry in America: Expression and its Value.* Durham, N.C.: Duke University Press, 1978.

Easthope, Antony. *Poetry as Discourse.* New York: Methuen, 1983.

————. "Traditional Metre and the Poetry of the Thirties." *Proceedings of the Essex Conference on the Sociology of Literature; July 1978.* Vol. 2. University of Essex, 1979. 324–43.

Eastman, Max. "Lazy Verse." *The New Republic,* 9 September 1916, 138–40.

Eberwein, Jane Donahue. *Dickinson: Strategies of Limitation.* Amherst: University of Massachusetts Press, 1985.

————. "Doing Without: Dickinson as Yankee Woman Poet." *Critical Essays on Emily Dickinson.* Ed. Paul J. Ferlazzo. Boston: Hall, 1984. 205–22.

Eichenbaum, Boris. "The Theory of the 'Formal Method.'" *Russian Formalist Essays: Four Essays.* Trans. Lee T. Lemon and Marion J. Reis. Lincoln: University of Nebraska Press, 1965. 99–139.

Eliot, T. S. "The Art of Poetry, I: T. S. Eliot." *Paris Review* 21 (1959): 46–70.

————. "The Borderline of Prose." *The New Statesman,* 19 May 1917, 157–59.

————. *The Complete Poems and Plays: 1909–1950.* New York: Harcourt, Brace and Co., 1952.

————. "Ezra Pound: His Metric and Poetry." 1917. *Modern Poetry: Essays in Criticism.* Ed. John Hollander. Oxford: Oxford University Press, 1968. 35–53.

————. "Milton II." *Selected Prose of T. S. Eliot.* Ed. Frank Kermode. Harcourt, Brace, Jovanovich, 1975. 265–74.

————. "The Music of Poetry." 1942. *On Poetry and Poets.* New York: Noonday Press, 1961. 17–33.

————. Preface. *Anabase.* By St.-J. Perse. Trans. T. S. Eliot. New York: Brentano's, 1945. 62–65.

————. "Reflections on Vers Libre." 1917. *Selected Prose of T. S. Eliot.* Ed. Frank Kermode. Harcourt, Brace, Jovanovich, 1975. 31–36.

————. "Swinburne as Poet." *Selected Essays.* New York: Harcourt, Brace and Co., 1950. 281–85.

————. "Talk on Dante." *Adelphi* 27 (1951): 104–12.

————. *The Use of Poetry and the Use of Criticism: Studies in the Relation of Criticism to Poetry in England.* London: Faber and Faber, 1933.

Emerson, Ralph Waldo. "The Poet." 1844. *Emerson's Essays.* New York: Crowell, 1926. 261–91.

Esenwein, J. Berg, and Mary Eleanor Roberts. *The Art of Versification.* Springfield, Mass.: Home Correspondence School, 1920.

Ficke, Arthur Davidson. "Metrical Freedom and the Contemporary Poet." *The Dial,* 1 January 1915, 11–13.

Fish, Stanley. "What Is Stylistics and Why Are They Saying Such Terrible Things About It?" *Approaches to Aesthetics.* Ed. Seymour Chatman. New York: Columbia University Press, 1973. 109–52.

Fletcher, John Gould. "Miss Lowell's Discovery: Polyphonic Prose." *Poetry* 6, no. 1 (April 1915): 32–36.

Folsom, Ed. "Talking Back to Walt Whitman: An Introduction." In Perlman xxi–liii.

Freedman, Morris. "Jazz Rhythms and T. S. Eliot." *South Atlantic Quarterly* 51 (1952): 419–35.

Frye, Northrop. *Anatomy of Criticism: Four Essays.* Princeton: Princeton University Press, 1957.

————. *T. S. Eliot.* Edinburgh: Oliver and Boyd, 1963.

Fuller, Henry. "A New Field for Free Verse." *The Dial,* 14 December 1916, 515–17.

Fuller, Roy. "L'Oncle Tom: Some Notes and Queries." *Agenda* 23, nos. 1–2 (1985): 41–52.

Fussell, Edwin. *Lucifer in Harness: American Meter, Metaphor, and Diction.* Princeton: Princeton University Press, 1973.

Fussell, Paul, Jr. "A Note on Samuel Johnson and the Rise of Accentual Prosodic Theory." *Philological Quarterly* 33 (1954): 431–33.

————. *Poetic Meter and Poetic Form.* New York: Random House, 1965.

————. *Theory of Prosody in Eighteenth-Century England.* Hamden, Conn.: Archon Books, 1966.

Gardner, Helen. *The Art of T. S. Eliot.* London: Cresset Press, 1949.

Garnett, Richard. "On Translating Homer." *Essays of an Ex-Librarian.* New York: Dodd, Mead, 1901.

Gascoigne, George. "Certayne Notes of Instruction." 1575. *Elizabethan Critical Essays.* Vol. 1. Ed. Gregory G. Smith. Oxford: Clarendon Press, 1904. 46–57.

Gates, Rosemary L. "The Identity of American Free Verse: The Prosodic Study of Whitman's 'Lilacs.'" *Language and Style* 18, no. 3 (1985): 248–76.

Gelpi, Albert. *The Tenth Muse: The Psyche of the American Poet.* Cambridge: Harvard University Press, 1975.

Gilbert, Sandra M., and Susan Gubar. *The Madwoman in the Attic: The Woman Writer and the Nineteenth-Century Literary Imagination.* New Haven: Yale University Press, 1979.

————. *No Man's Land: The Place of the Woman Writer in the Twentieth Century* Vol. 1: *The War of the Words.* New Haven: Yale University Press, 1987.

————, eds. *The Norton Anthology of Literature by Women: The Tradition in English.* New York: Norton, 1985.

Gingell, Susan. "Prosodic Signification in the Longer Poems of Klein's *Hath Not a Jew.*" *Canadian Poetry* 19 (1986): 11–25.

Ginsberg, Allen. *Howl.* San Francisco: City Lights Books, 1956.

Gioia, Dana. "Longfellow in the Aftermath of Modernism." *Columbia History of American Poetry.* Ed. Jay Parini. New York: Columbia University Press, 1993.

Gish, Nancy K. *The Waste Land: A Poem of Memory and Desire.* Boston: Twayne, 1988.

Glowka, Arthur Wayne. "The Function of Meter According to Ancient and Medieval Theory." *Allegorica* 7, no.2 (1982): 100–109.

Grahn, Judy. "Like a woman in childbirth wailing." *The Queen of Wands.* Trumansburg, N.Y.: The Crossing Press, 1982. 68–73.

Graves, Robert. *Contemporary Techniques of Poetry: A Political Analogy.* London: Hogarth Press, 1925.

Greenblatt, Daniel L. "The Effect of Genre on Metrical Style." *Language and Style* 11 (1978): 18–29.

Gregory, Horace. *Amy Lowell: Portrait of the Poet in Her Time.* New York: Thomas Nelson and Sons, 1958.

Griffin, Clark. *The Long Shadow.* Princeton: Princeton University Press, 1964.

Gross, Harvey. *Sound and Form in Modern Poetry: A Study of Prosody from Thomas Hardy to Robert Lowell.* Ann Arbor: University of Michigan Press, 1964.

Gross, Kenneth. "'Each Heav'nly Close': Mythologies and Metrics in Spenser and the Early Poetry of Milton." *PMLA* 98, no.1 (1973): 21–36.

Guest, Barbara. *Herself Defined: The Poet H.D. and Her World.* London: Collins, 1985.

Gummere, Francis B. *The Beginnings of Poetry.* New York: Macmillan, 1901.

————. *Democracy and Poetry.* Boston: Houghton Mifflin, 1911.

————. *A Handbook of Poetics for Students of English Verse.* Boston: Ginn & Company, 1890.

Hale, Edward Everett. Review of *Leaves of Grass. North American Review* 82 (January 1856): 275–77. Rpt. in Woodress 21–23.

Hall, W. Winslow. *English Poesy: An Induction.* London: J. M. Dent and Sons, 1911.

Halle, Morris, and Samuel Jay Keyser. "The Iambic Pentameter." *Versification: Major Language Types.* Ed. W. K. Wimsatt. New York: New York University Press, 1972. 217–37.

Halliburton, David. *The Color of the Sky: A Study of Stephen Crane.* Cambridge: Cambridge University Press, 1989.

Halpern, Martin. "On the Two Chief Metrical Modes in English." *PMLA* 77, no.3 (1962): 177–86.

Hamm, Victor. "Meter and Meaning." *PMLA* 69 (1954): 695–710.

Hart, James M. "The College Course in English Literature, How it May Be Improved." *PMLA* 1 (1884–85): 84–95.

Hartman, Charles O. *Free Verse: An Essay on Prosody*. Princeton: Princeton University Press, 1980.

Henderson, Alice Corbin. "Convention and Revolt." *Poetry* 14, no. 5 (August 1919): 269–73.

———. "Lazy Criticism." *Poetry* 9, no. 3 (December 1916): 144–49.

———. "Mannerisms of Free Verse." *Poetry* 14, no. 2 (May 1919): 95–98.

———. "A Perfect Return." *Poetry* 1, no. 2 (November 1912): 86–91.

Hewitt, Elizabeth. "Structure and Meaning in T. S. Eliot's 'Ash Wednesday'." *Anglia* 83 (1965): 426–50.

Higginson, Thomas Wentworth. Review of *The Black Riders and Other Lines*, by Stephen Crane. *Nation* 24 (October 1895). Rpt. in Weatherford 67–70.

Hindus, Milton. "Notes towards the Definition of a Typical Poetic Line in Whitman." *Walt Whitman Review* 9, no. 4 (1963): 75–81.

———, ed. *Walt Whitman: The Critical Heritage*. New York: Barnes and Noble, 1971.

Hoffman, Daniel G. *The Poetry of Stephen Crane*. New York: Columbia University Press, 1957.

Hollander, John. *Melodious Guile: Fictive Pattern in Poetic Language*. New Haven: Yale University Press, 1988.

———. *Vision and Resonance: Two Senses of Poetic Form*. 1975. 2d ed. New Haven: Yale University Press, 1985.

Homans, Margaret. "Oh, Vision of Language: Dickinson's Poems on Love and Death." *Feminist Critics Read Emily Dickinson*. Ed. Suzanne Juhasz. Bloomington: Indiana University Press, 1983. 114–33.

———. *Women Writers and Poetic Identity*. Princeton University Press, 1980.

Hopkins, Gerard Manley. *The Letters of Gerard Manley Hopkins to Robert Bridges*. Ed. Claude Colleer Abbott. London: Oxford University Press, 1935. 154–58. Rpt. in Woodress 135–37.

Howells, William Dean. Review of *The Black Riders and Other Lines*, by Stephen Crane. *Harper's Weekly*. 25 January 1896. Rpt. in Weatherford 70–72.

———. Review of *Drum Taps*, by Walt Whitman. *The Round Table*, (11 November 1865), 147–48. Rpt. in Woodress 56–58.

Hubbard, Elbert. Review of *The Black Riders and Other Lines*, by Stephen Crane. *Roycraft Quarterly*, May 1896. Rpt. in Weatherford 75–80.

Hughes, Glenn. *Imagism and the Imagists: A Study in Modern Poetry*. 1931. New York: Biblo and Tannen, 1972.

Hunt, Leigh. *What Is Poetry?* 1844. Ed. Albert S. Cook. Boston: Ginn and Co., 1893.

Isaacs, J. *The Background of Modern Poetry*. New York: Dutton, 1952.

Jacob, Mark. "The Semantic Role of Metre in Pushkin's *Zimny Vecher*: A Suitable Case for Analysis?" *Essays in Poetics: The Journal of the British Neo-Formalist School* 10, no. 1 (1985): 81–98.

Jay, Gregory S. "Ghosts and Roses." *T. S. Eliot*. Ed. Harold Bloom. New York: Chelsea House, 1985. 103–19.

Johnson, Samuel. "Life of Cowley." *Lives of the English Poets*. Vol. 1. Ed. George Burbank Hill. Oxford: Clarendon Press, 1905. 1–69.

————. *The Rambler, The Yale Edition of the Works of Samuel Johnson*. Vol.4: *The Rambler*. Ed. W. J. Bate and A. B. Straus. New Haven: Yale University Press, 1969. 121–43.

Johnson, Thomas. *Emily Dickinson: An Interpretative Biography*. Cambridge: Harvard University Press, 1955.

Jones, Llewellyn. "Free Verse and Its Propaganda." *Sewanee Review* 28 (July 1920): 384–95.

Juhasz, Suzanne. *Naked and Fiery Forms: Modern American Poetry by American Women, A New Tradition*. New York: Harper, 1976.

————. *The Undiscovered Continent: Emily Dickinson and the Space of the Mind*. Bloomington: Indiana University Press, 1983.

Kammer, Jeanne. "The Art of Silence and the Forms of Women's Poetry." *Shakespeare's Sisters: Feminist Essays on Women Poets*. Ed. Sandra M. Gilbert and Susan Gubar. Bloomington: Indiana University Press, 1979. 153–64.

Keller, Karl. *The Only Kangaroo among the Beauty: Emily Dickinson and America*. Baltimore: Johns Hopkins University Press, 1979.

Kenner, Hugh. *Invisible Poet: T. S. Eliot*. New York: McDowell, Obolensky, 1959.

Kilmer, Joyce. *Literature in the Making*. New York: Harper, 1917.

Kindilien, Carlin T. *American Poetry in the 1890s*. Providence: Brown University Press, 1956.

Koch, Kenneth. *Wishes, Lies, and Dreams: Teaching Children to Write Poetry*. New York: Harper, 1970.

Lanier, Sidney. "The Science of English Verse." 1880. *The Centennial Edition of the Works of Sidney Lanier*. Vol. 2. Ed. Paul Franklin Baum. Baltimore: Johns Hopkins University Press, 1945. 1–244.

Lawrence, D. H. "Whitman." *Nation and Athenaeum* 29 (July 1921): 616–18. Rpt. in *Leaves of Grass*, by Walt Whitman. Ed. Sculley Bradley and Harold W. Blodgett. New York: Norton, 1973. 842–50.

Leavis, F. R. *New Bearings in English Poetry: A Study of the Contemporary Situation*. Ann Arbor: Univeristy of Michigan Press, 1932.

Levy, Jiri. "Rhythmical Ambivalence in the Poetry of T. S. Eliot." *Anglia* 77 (1959): 54–64.

Lewis, Kevin. "Prophetic Vision and the Metrical Contract: The Rhetoric of Meter in William Blake's *Jerusalem* and W. H. Auden's *New Year Letter*." Diss. University of Chicago Divinity School, 1980.

Leyda, Jay. *The Years and Hours of Emily Dickinson*. 2 vols. New Haven: Yale University Press, 1960.

Lindberg-Seyersted, Brita. *The Voice of the Poet: Aspects of Style in the Poetry of Emily Dickinson*. Cambridge: Harvard University Press, 1968.

Lobb, Edward. *T. S. Eliot and the Romantic Critical Tradition*. London: Routledge and Kegan Paul, 1981.

Lorde, Audre. *The Black Unicorn*. New York: Norton, 1978.

Lotman, Juri. *Analysis of the Poetic Text*. Ed. and trans. D. Barton Johnson. Ann Arbor, Michigan: Ardis, 1976.

Lowell, Amy. *Tendencies in Modern American Poetry*. New York: MacMillan, 1917.

Lucy, Sean. *T. S. Eliot and the Idea of Tradition*. London: Cohen and West, 1960.

Masters, Edgar Lee. "Petit, the Poet." *Spoon River Anthology*. 1915. New York: Collier, 1966. 109.

Matthiessen, F. O. *American Renaissance: Art and Expression in the Age of Emerson and Whitman*. London, Oxford University Press, 1941.

Menard, Louis. *Discovering Modernism: T. S. Eliot and His Context*. New York: Oxford University Press, 1987.

Middlebrook, Diane. *Anne Sexton: A Biography*. Boston: Houghton Mifflin, 1991.

Miller, Cristanne. "How 'Low Feet' Stagger: Disruptions of Language in Dickinson's Poetry." *Feminist Critics Read Emily Dickinson*. Ed. Suzanne Juhasz. Bloomington: Indiana University Press, 1983. 134–55.

Miller, Edwin H, ed. *A Century of Whitman Criticism*. Bloomington: Indiana University Press, 1969.

Miller, J. Hillis. *Poets of Reality: Six Twentieth-Century Writers*. Cambridge: Belknap Press of Harvard University Press, 1965.

Miller, James E. *A Critical Guide to Leaves of Grass*. Chicago: University of Chicago Press, 1957.

Miller, Ruth. *The Poetry of Emily Dickinson*. Middletown: Wesleyan University Press, 1968.

Mitchell, Roger. "A Prosody for Whitman?" *PMLA* 84 (1969): 1606–12.

Monroe, Harriet. "Down East." *Poetry* 8, no. 2 (May 1916): 85–89.

———. "Dr. Patterson on Rhythm." *Poetry* 12, no. 1 (April 1918): 30–36.

———. "Its Inner Meaning." *Poetry* 6, no. 6 (September 1915): 302–05.

———. "Men or Women?" *Poetry* 16, no. 4 (June 1920): 146–48.

———. "Notes." *Poetry* 22, no. 6 (September 1923): 346–48.

———. "Notes and Announcements." *Poetry* 1, no. 2 (November 1912): 64–65.

———. "On the Reading of Poetry." *Poetry* 1, no. 1 (October 1912): 22–25.

———. *Poets and Their Art*. 1932. Freeport, New York: Books for Libraries Press, 1967.

———. "A Staccato Poet." *Poetry* 9, no. 1 (October 1916): 51–54.

———. "Various Views." *Poetry* 8, no. 3 (June 1916): 140–44.

———. "What Next?" *Poetry* 15 (October 1919): 33–38.

Moore, Charles Leonard. "The Lost Art of Blank Verse." *The Dial*, 16 November 1902, 317–19.

More, Paul Elmer. "Walt Whitman." *Shelburne Essays on American Literature*. Ed. Daniel Aaron. New York: Harcourt, 1963. 230–53.

Mossberg, Barbara. *Emily Dickinson: When a Writer Is a Daughter*. Bloomington: Indiana University Press, 1982.

Musgrove, Samuel. *T. S. Eliot and Walt Whitman*. Wellington: University of New Zealand Press, 1952.

Nabokov, Vladimir. "Notes on Prosody." *Notes on Prosody and Abram Gannibal*. Princeton: Princeton University Press, 1964. 3–95.

Nemerov. Howard. "One Last Midrash." *Reflexions on Poetry and Poetics*. New Brunswick: Rutgers University Press, 1972.

Nevo, Ruth. *"The Waste Land: Ur*-Text of Deconstruction." *T. S. Eliot*. Ed. Harold Bloom. New York: Chelsea House, 1985. 95–102.

North, Jessica Nelson. "The Late Rebellion: By One of its Pall-Bearers." *Poetry* 12, no. 3 (June 1923): 153–56.

Norton, Charles Eliot. Review of *Leaves of Grass. Putnum's Monthly* 6 (September 1855): 321–23. Rpt. in Woodress 19–21.

O'Conor, Norreys Jephson. "A New Book on Poetics." *Poetry* 12, no. 4 (July 1923): 218–21.

Omond, T. S. "Is Verse a Trammel?" *The Gentleman's Magazine* n.s. 14 (1875): 344–54.

Palmer, George Herbert. "Hexameters and Rhythmic Prose." *The Atlantic Monthly* 66 (1890): 526–34.

Pearce, Roy Harvey. *The Continuity of American Poetry*. Princeton: Princeton University Press, 1961.

Peck, Harry Thurston. Review of *The Black Riders and Other Lines*, by Stephen Crane. *Bookman* May 1895. Rpt. in Weatherford 63–65.

Perkins, David. *A History of Modern Poetry: From the 1890s to the High Modernist Mode*. Cambridge: Belknap Press of Harvard University Press, 1976.

Perlman, Jim, Ed Folsom, and Dan Campion, eds. *Walt Whitman: The Measure of His Song*. Minneapolis, Holy Cow! Press, 1981.

Perry, Bliss. *Walt Whitman: His Life and Works*. Boston: Houghton, 1906.

Plato. "Republic." Trans. Paul Shorey. *The Collected Dialogues of Plato*. Ed. Edith Hamilton and Huntington Cairns. Princeton: Princeton University Press, 1961. 575–844.

Poe, Edgar Allan. "The Rationale of Verse." *The Miscellaneous Essays of Edgar Allan Poe*. Ed. James A. Harrison. New York: Crowell, 1902. 209–65.

Pollak, Vivian. "Emily Dickinson's Valentines." *American Quarterly* 26 (1974): 60–78.

Pope, Alexander. *The Poems of Alexander Pope*. Ed. John Butt. New Haven: Yale University Press, 1963.

Porter, David T. *The Art of Emily Dickinson's Early Poetry*. Cambridge: Harvard University Press, 1966.

Pound, Ezra. "Harold Monro." *Criterion* 11 (July 1932): 590.

———. "A Retrospect." 1918. *Literary Essays of Ezra Pound*. Ed. T. S. Eliot. New York: New Directions, 1968. 3–14.

———. "T. S. Eliot." 1917. *Literary Essays of Ezra Pound*. Ed. T. S. Eliot. New York: New Directions, 1968. 418–22.

———. "Vers Libre and Arnold Dolmetsch." 1918. *Literary Essays of Ezra Pound*. Ed. T. S. Eliot. New York: New Directions, 1968. 437–40.

Princeton Encyclopedia of Poetry and Poetics. Ed. Alex Preminger. Princeton: Princeton University Press, 1974.

Ransom, John Crowe. "Dickinson's Poetic Personality." *Critics on Emily Dickinson*. Ed. Richard H. Rupp. Coral Gables: University of Miami Press, 1972. 30–33.

————. "Wanted: An Ontological Critic." *Beating the Bushes: Selected Essays 1941–1970.* New York: New Directions, 1972. 1–46.

Raven, David. *Greek Metre: An Introduction.* 2d ed. London: Faber, 1968.

Raymond, George L. *Poetry as a Representative Art.* New York: G. P. Putnam's Sons, 1885.

Rees, Thomas R. *The Technique of T. S. Eliot: A Study of the Orchestration of Meaning in Eliot's Poetry.* The Hague: Mouton, 1974.

"Reflections: Mr. Eliot." *Time,* 6 March 1950: 22–26.

Reibetanz, Julia M. "Traditional Meters in Four Quartets." *English Studies* 56 (1975): 409–20.

Review of *The Black Riders and Other Lines,* by Stephen Crane. *Munsey's Magazine,* July 1895. Rpt. in Weatherford 66–67.

Review of *The Black Riders and Other Lines,* by Stephen Crane. *New York Daily Tribune* 9 June 1895. Rpt. in Weatherford 65–66.

Review of *Leaves of Grass. Critic* [London] 15 (April 1856): 170–71. Rpt. in Woodress 41–43.

Review of *Leaves of Grass. New York Tribune* 19 November 1881. Rpt. in Woodress 71–72.

Richards, I. A. *Practical Criticism: A Study of Literary Judgement.* New York: Harcourt, Brace, 1929.

————. *Principles of Literary Criticism.* New York: Harcourt, Brace, 1925.

Robertson, John M. "Form in Poetry." *English Review* 8 (1911): 377–97.

Ross, E. C. "Whitman's Verse." *Modern Language Notes* 34 (1930): 363–64.

Rukeyser, Muriel. "Whitman and the Problem of Good." *The Life of Poetry.* 1949. Rpt. in Perlman 102–10.

Saintsbury, George. *Historical Manual of English Prosody.* 1910. New York: Schocken Books, 1966.

————. *A History of English Prosody from the Twelfth Century to the Present Day.* Vol. 3. London: Macmillan, 1906–10. New York: Russell and Russell, 1961. 3 vols.

————. Review of *Leaves of Grass. The Academy* [London], 10 October 1874, 298–400. Rpt. in *Leaves of Grass,* by Walt Whitman. Ed. Sculley Bradley and Harold W. Blodgett. New York: Norton, 1973. 782–90.

Schiller, Andrew. "An Approach to Whitman's Metrics." *Emerson Society Quarterly* 22 (1961): 23–25.

Scott, Fred Newton. "The Most Fundamental Differentia of Poetry and Prose." *PMLA* 19 (1904): 250–69.

————. "A Note on Walt Whitman's Prosody." *Journal of English and Germanic Philology* 7, no. 2 (1908): 134–53.

Sewall, Richard B. *The Life of Emily Dickinson.* 2 vols. New York: Farrar, 1974.

Sexton, Anne. *Anne Sexton: A Self-Portrait in Letters.* Ed. Linda Gray Sexton and Lois Ames. Boston: Houghton Mifflin, 1979.

————. *Complete Poems of Anne Sexton.* Boston: Houghton Mifflin, 1981.

Shapiro, James S. "Marlowe's Metrical Style: 'Infinite Riches in a Little Roome.'" Diss. University of Chicago, 1982.

Shephard, Esther. "An Inquiry into Whitman's Method of Turning Prose into Poetry." *Modern Language Quarterly* 14 (1953): 43–59.

Shucard, Alan, Fred Moramarco, and William Sullivan, eds. *Modern American Poetry: 1865–1950*. Boston: Twanye, 1989.

Sidney, Philip. "The Defense of Poesie." *Elizabethan Critical Essays*. Vol. 1. Ed. Gregory G. Smith. Oxford: Clarendon Press, 1904. 148–207.

Sims, D. L. "Rhythm and Meaning." *Essays in Criticism* 6 (1956): 347–52.

Smith, Barbara Herrnstein. *Poetic Closure: A Study of How Poems End*. Chicago: University of Chicago Press, 1968.

Sokolsky, Anita. "The Resistance to Sentimentality: Yeats, de Man, and the Aesthetic Education." *Yale Journal of Criticism* 1, no. 1 (1987): 67–86.

Soldo, John J. "T. S. Eliot and Jules LaForgue." *American Literature* 55, no. 2 (May 1983): 137–50.

Southey, Robert. "Preface." *A Vision of Judgement*. 1821. *The Poetical Works of Robert Southey*. Vol. 10. London: Longman, Orme, Brown, Greer, and Longmans, 1838. 422–36. 10 vols.

St. Armand, Barton Levi. *Emily Dickinson and Her Culture*. Cambridge: Cambridge University Press, 1984.

Stanford, Derek, and Julie Whitby. "Three Readings of T. S. Eliot: Clio, Melpomene, Euterpe." *Agenda* 23, nos. 1–2 (1985): 72–81.

Stanford, Donald E. *Revolution and Convention in Modern Poetry: Studies in Ezra Pound, T. S. Eliot, Wallace Stevens, Edwin Arlington Robinson, and Yvor Winters*. Newark: University of Delaware Press, 1983.

Stauffer, Donald Barlow. *A Short History of American Poetry*. New York: Dutton, 1974.

Stead, C. K. *Pound, Yeats, Eliot and the Modernist Movement*. London: MacMillan, 1986.

Stedman, Edmund Clarence. "Introduction." *An American Anthology: 1787–1900*. Boston: Houghton Mifflin, 1900. xv–xxxiv.

———. Review of *Leaves of Grass*. *Scribner's* 21 (November 1880): 47–64. Rpt. in Woodress 116–27.

Steele, Timothy. *Missing Measures: Modern Poetry and The Revolt Against Meter*. Fayetteville: University of Arkansas Press, 1990.

Stefanile, Felix. "The Maligning of Walt Whitman." *PN Review* 16, no. 3 (1989): 8–9.

Stevenson, Robert Louis. "The Gospel According to Walt Whitman." *Familiar Studies of Men and Books*. London: Cassell and Co., 1882. xvii–xix, 91–128. Rpt. in Woodress 109–15.

Storer, Edward. "Form in Free Verse." *New Republic*, 11 March 1916, 154–56.

Svarny, Erik. *"The Men of 1914": T. S. Eliot and Early Modernism*. Philadelphia: Open University Press, 1988.

Swinburne, Algernon Charles. "Whitmania." *Fortnightly Review* 1887. Rpt. in Hindus 199–207.

Szerdahelyi, Istvan. "The Semantics of Rhythm in Verse (On the Problems of Content in Abstract Forms)." *Acta Litteraria Academiae Scientiarum Hungaricae* 25, nos. 1–2 (1983): 69–89.

Tarlinskaja, Marina. "Rhythm and Meaning: 'Rhythmical Figures' in English Iambic Pentameter, Their Grammar, and Their Links with Semantics." *Style* 21, no. 1 (1987): 1–35.

Taylor, Dennis. *Hardy's Meters and Victorian Prosody; with a metrical appendix of his stanza forms*. Oxford: Clarendon Press, 1988.

Thayer, William Roscoe. "Personal Recollections of Walt Whitman." *Scribner's Magazine* 65 (June 1919): 674–87. Rpt. in *Whitman, Bryant, Melville and Holmes Among Their Contemporaries: A Harvest of Estimates, Insights, and Anecdotes from the Victorian Literary World and an Index*. Ed. Kenneth Walter Cameron. Hartford: Transcendental Books, 1976. 484–90.

Thompson, John. *The Founding of English Meter*. New York: Columbia University Press, 1961.

Tsur, Reuven. "Contrast, Ambiguity, Double-Edgedness." *Poetics Today* 6, no. 3 (1985): 417–45.

Upward, Allen. "The Discarded Imagist." *Poetry* 6, no. 6 (September 1915): 317–18.

Walker, Cheryl. *The Nightingale's Burden: Women Poets and American Culture before 1900*. Bloomington: Indiana University Press, 1982.

Walker, Robert H. *The Poet and the Gilded Age: Social Themes in Late 19th Century American Verse*. Philadelphia: University of Pennsylvania Press, 1963.

Walsh, John Evangelist. *The Hidden Life of Emily Dickinson*. New York: Simon, 1971.

Ware, Lois. "Poetic Conventions in *Leaves of Grass*." *Studies in Philology* 26 (January 1929): 47–57.

Warren, Austin. "Eliot's Literary Criticism." *T. S. Eliot: The Man and His Work*. Ed. Allen Tate. New York: Delacorte Press, 1966. 278–98.

Warton, Thomas. *The History of English Poetry*. Vol. 3. London: J. Dodsley, 1774–81. 3 vols.

Watts, Emily Stipes. *The Poetry of American Women from 1632 to 1945*. Austin: University of Texas Press, 1977.

Weatherford, Richard M., ed. *Stephen Crane: The Critical Heritage*. London: Routledge and Kegan Paul, 1973.

Weissmuller, Edward. "Triple Threats to Duple Rhythm." *Phonetics and Phonology*. Vol. 3: *Rhythm and Meter*. Ed. Paul Kiparsky and Gilbert Youmans. San Diego: Academic Press, 1989. 261–90.

Wellek, Rene. *A History of Modern Criticism: 1750–1950*. Vol. 4: *The Later Nineteenth Century*. New Haven: Yale University Press, 1965. 4 vols.

Wendell, Barrett. *The Literary History of America*. New York: Scribner's, 1931.

Whicher, George Frisbie. *This Was a Poet: A Critical Biography of Emily Dickinson*. Ann Arbor: University of Michigan Press, 1957.

Whitman, Walt. *Leaves of Grass*. Ed. Sculley Bradley and Harold W. Blodgett. New York: Norton, 1973.

———. *Specimen Days and Collect*. Philadelphia: David McKay, 1882.

———. "A Thought on Shakespeare." *November Boughs*. *Walt Whitman: The Complete Poetry and Prose*. Ed. Justin Kaplan. New York: The Library of America, 1982.

Wilbur, Richard. "Sumptuous Destitution." *Emily Dickinson: 3 Views*. Amherst: Amherst College Press, 1960. 35–46.

Williams, William Carlos. "An Essay on *Leaves of Grass*." *Whitman: A Collection of Critical Essays*. Ed. Roy Harvey Pearce. Englewood Cliffs, N. J.: Prentice, 1962. 146–54.

———. "Letter to Kay Boyle." 1932. *American Poetic Theory*. Ed. George Perkins. New York: Holt, Rinehart and Winston, 1972. 264–71.

———. *Selected Essays of William Carlos Williams*. New York: Random House, 1954.

Winter, D. "Verse and Prose." *Journal of English and Germanic Philology* 5 (1903–5): 271–86.

Winters, Yvor. "The Audible Reading of Poetry." *The Structure of Verse*. Ed. Harvey Gross. New York: Ecco Press, 1979. 129–46.

Wolosky, Shira. *Emily Dickinson: A Voice of War*. New Haven: Yale University Press, 1984.

Wood, Clement. *Poets' Handbook*. Cleveland: World Publishing Co., 1940.

Woodress, James, ed. *Critical Essays on Walt Whitman*. Boston: G. K. Hall, 1983.

Wordsworth, William. "Preface." *Lyrical Ballads*. 1802. *The Prose Works of William Wordsworth*. Vol. 1. Ed. W. J. B. Owen and Jane Worthington Smyser. Oxford: Clarendon Press, 1974. 118–59.

Wright, Charles. *The World of the Ten Thousand Things*. New York: Farrar Straus, 1990.

Wright, James. "The Delicacy of Walt Whitman." *The Presence of Walt Whitman*. Ed. R. W. B. Lewis. New York: Columbia University Press, 1962. Rpt. in Perlman 161–76.

Zaturenska, Marya. *Christina Rossetti*. New York: MacMillan, 1949.

Ziff, Larzer. *The American 1890s: Life and Times of a Lost Generation*. New York: Viking Press, 1966.

Index